THE 21 IRREFUTABLE LAWS OF LEADERSHIP WORKBOOK

THE 21 IRREFUTABLE LAWS OF LEADERSHIP

WORKBOOK

JOHN C. MAXWELL

THOMAS NELSON PUBLISHERS®
Nashville

A Division of Thomas Nelson, Inc.
www.ThomasNelson.com

Published in Nashville, Tennessee, by Thomas Nelson, Inc.

ISBN 0-7852-6405-1

Printed in the United States of America

04 05 06 BVG 5 4 3

CONTENTS

INTRODUCTION

As I travel and speak to organizations and individuals, people frequently ask me to define the essentials of leadership. "If you were to take everything you've learned about leadership over the years and boil it down into a short list," they ask, "what would it be?"

This workbook contains my answer to that often-asked question. It has taken me a lifetime to learn these 21 Irrefutable Laws of Leadership. And now I'm getting the opportunity to present them in a workbook format. My desire is to communicate them to you as simply and clearly as possible. And it sure wouldn't hurt if we have some fun along the way.

One of the most important truths I've learned over the years is this: Leadership is leadership, no matter where you go or what you do. Times change. Technology marches forward. Cultures vary from place to place. But the true principles of leadership are constant—whether you're looking at the citizens of ancient Greece, the Hebrews in the Old Testament, the armies of the last two hundred years, the rulers of modern Europe, the pastors in local churches, or the businesspeople of today's global economy. Leadership principles stand the test of time. They are irrefutable.

As you make your way through this workbook, I'd like you to keep in mind four ideas:

1. **The laws can be learned.** Some laws are easier to understand and apply than others, but every one of them can be acquired.

2. **The laws can stand alone.** Each law complements all the others, but you don't need one in order to learn another.

3. **The laws carry consequences with them.** Apply the laws, and people will follow you. Violate or ignore them, and you will not be able to lead others.

4. **The laws are the foundations of leadership.** Once you learn the principles, you have to practice them and apply them to your life.

This workbook has been written with the goal of helping you to accomplish the task of practicing and applying the laws. In the following pages I will challenge you to take a hard look at each law and how it applies to your life and leadership potential. By answering questions and participating in activities, you will begin to identify how these laws affect your success and the success of the people in areas of your life, such as family, work, volunteer organizations, or social circles.

Each law includes stories that will help you observe the law in action, questions to evaluate your own level of leadership, discussion questions to see how a particular law affects your organization, and an action section where you can improve your leadership skills.

While most workbooks are designed in a weekly format that builds throughout the study, that is not the case with *The 21 Irrefutable Laws of Leadership Workbook.* As I have already mentioned, each law can stand on its own. And as you read about the laws, you may recognize that you already practice some of the principles effectively, or you may discover an area of weakness that you didn't know you had. For example you may already understand and apply the Law of Solid Ground, but you could benefit by taking a closer look at the Law of Empowerment. It's up to you where to start and how many laws to cover. This is your study. I encourage you to personalize it!

You can certainly learn the laws of leadership on your own using this workbook. However, since leadership is about working with people, this workbook has been set up so that groups can learn about the laws together. The first four sections (Read, Observe, Learn, Evaluate) are to be completed individually, and the last two sections (Discuss, Action) are best reviewed in a group setting. If you are leading a group through this workbook, you can find a leader's guide with additional suggestions and instructions for these two sections at www.MaximumImpact.com. Since individual members of the group will have different areas of strength and weakness, I suggest you work your way through the study covering each law. That way, members of the group can learn from each other while improving their leadership skills.

Whether you are a follower who is just beginning to discover the impact of leadership or a natural leader who already has followers, you can become a better leader. Each law is like a tool, ready to be picked up and used to help you achieve your dreams and add value to other people. Pick up even one, and you will become a better leader. Master them all, and people will gladly follow you.

Come on, let's open the toolbox and get started!

1

THE LAW OF THE LID

Leadership Ability Determines a Person's Level of Effectiveness

The *Law of the Lid* will help you understand the value of leadership. If you can get a handle on this law, you will see the incredible impact leadership has on every aspect of life.

READ

In 1930, two young brothers named Dick and Maurice moved from New Hampshire to California in search of the American dream. They had just gotten out of high school, and they saw few opportunities back home. So they headed straight for Hollywood where they eventually found jobs on a movie studio set.

After a while, their entrepreneurial spirit and interest in the entertainment industry prompted them to open a theater in Glendale, a town about five miles northeast of Hollywood. But despite all their efforts, the brothers just couldn't make the business profitable. In the four years they ran the theater, they weren't even able to consistently generate enough money to pay the $100 a month rent that their landlord required.

The brothers' desire for success was strong, so they kept looking for better business opportunities. In 1937 they finally struck on something that worked. They opened a small drive-in restaurant in Pasadena, located just east of Glendale. People in southern California had become very dependent on their cars, and the culture was changing to accommodate that, including its businesses.

Drive-in restaurants were a phenomenon that sprang up in the early thirties, and they were becoming very popular. Rather than being invited into a dining room to eat, customers would drive into a parking lot around a small restaurant, place their orders with carhops, and receive their food on trays right in their cars. The food was served on china plates complete with glassware and metal utensils. It was great idea in a society that was becoming faster-paced and increasingly mobile.

Dick and Maurice's tiny drive-in restaurant was a great success, and in 1940 they decided to move the operation to San Bernardino, a working-class boomtown fifty miles east of Los Angeles. They built a larger facility and expanded their menu from hot dogs, fries, and shakes to include barbecued beef and pork sandwiches, hamburgers, and other items. Their business exploded. Annual sales reached $200,000, and the brothers found themselves splitting $50,000 in profits every year—a sum that put them in the town's financial elite.

In 1948 their intuition told them that times were changing, and they made modifications to their restaurant business. They eliminated the carhops and starting serving only walk-up customers. And they also streamlined everything. They reduced their menu and focused on selling hamburgers. They eliminated plates, glassware, and metal utensils, switching to paper products instead. They reduced their costs and the prices they charged customers. They also created what they called the Speedy Service System. Their kitchen became like an assembly line, where each person focused on service with speed. Their goal was to fill each customer's order in thirty seconds or less. And they succeeded. By the mid 1950s annual revenue hit $350,000, and by then Dick and Maurice split net profits of about $100,000 each year.

Who were these brothers? Back in those days, you could have found out by driving by their small restaurant on the corner of Fourteenth and E streets in San Bernardino. On the front of the small octagonal building hung a neon sign that said simply "McDonald's Hamburgers." Dick and Maurice McDonald had hit the great American jackpot, and the rest, as they say, is history, right? Wrong. The McDonalds never went any further because their weak leadership put a lid on their ability to succeed.

It's true that the McDonald brothers were financially secure. Theirs was one of the most profitable restaurant enterprises in the country, and they felt that they had a hard time spending all the money they made. Their genius was in customer service and kitchen organization. That talent led to the creation of a new system of food and beverage service. In fact their talent was so widely known in food-service circles that people started writing them and visiting from all over the country to learn more about their methods. At one point they were receiving as many as 300 calls and letters every month.

That led them to the idea of marketing the McDonald's concept. The idea of franchising restaurants wasn't new. It had been around for several decades. To the McDonald brothers, it looked like a way to make money without having to open another restaurant themselves. In 1952 they got started, but their effort was a dismal failure. The reason was simple. They lacked the leadership necessary to make it effective. Dick and Maurice were good restaurant owners. They understood how to run a business, make their systems efficient, cut costs, and increase profits. They were good and efficient managers. But they were not leaders. Their thinking patterns clamped a lid down on what they could do and become. At the height of their success, Dick and Maurice found themselves smack dab against the *Law of the Lid*.

In 1954 the brothers hooked up with a man named Ray Kroc who *was* a leader. Kroc had been running a small company he founded that sold machines for making milk shakes. He had heard about McDonald's. In fact their restaurant was one of his best customers. And as soon as he visited the store, he had a vision for its potential. In his mind he could see the restaurant going nationwide in hundreds of markets. He soon struck a deal with Dick and Maurice, and in 1955 he formed McDonald's System, Inc. (later called the McDonald's Corporation).

One of the first things he did was buy the rights to a franchise himself so that he could use it as a model and prototype to sell other franchises. Then he began to assemble a team and build an organization to make McDonald's a nationwide entity. He recruited and hired the sharpest people he could find, and as his team grew in size and ability, his people began to develop additional recruits who had leadership skill.

In the early years Kroc sacrificed a lot. Though he was in his midfifties, he worked long hours just as he had when he first got started in business thirty years before. He eliminated many frills at home, including his country club membership, which he later said added ten strokes to his golf game. In fact, during his first eight years with McDonald's, he took no salary. Not only that, but he personally borrowed money from the bank and against his life insurance to help cover the salaries of a few key leaders he wanted on the team. His sacrifice and his leadership paid off. In 1961 for the sum of $2.7 million, Kroc bought the exclusive rights to McDonald's from the brothers and proceeded to turn it into an American institution and global entity. The "lid" in the life and leadership of Ray Kroc was obviously much higher than that of his predecessors.

In the years that Dick and Maurice McDonald had attempted to franchise their food-service system, they managed to sell the concept to just fifteen buyers, only ten of whom actually opened restaurants. And even in that small enterprise, their limited leadership and vision were hindrances. For example when their first franchisee, Neil Fox of Phoenix, told the brothers that he wanted to call his restaurant McDonald's, Dick's response was, "What the . . . for? McDonald's means nothing in Phoenix."

On the other hand the leadership lid in Ray Kroc's life was sky high. Between 1955 and 1959, Kroc succeeded in opening 100 restaurants. Four years after that, there were 500 McDonald's. Today the company has opened more than 21,000 restaurants in no fewer than 100 countries.[1]

OBSERVE

Leadership ability is the lid that determines a person's level of effectiveness. The lower an individual's ability to lead, the lower the lid on his or her potential. The higher the leadership, the greater the effectiveness.

Leadership ability—or more specifically the lack of leadership ability—was the lid to the McDonald brothers' effectiveness.

1. *Give two examples of steps Ray Kroc took to build the franchise business that the McDonald brothers didn't take.*

2. *How did these actions reflect Ray Kroc's leadership ability?*

3. *From your profession or area of service, give an example of a leader who has been limited by his or her "lid." How has this leader's "lid" affected the organization?*

4. *Whom do you know whose leadership lid seems unlimited?*

LEARN

Whatever you will accomplish is restricted by your ability to lead others. For example, if your leadership could be rated as an 8, then your effectiveness can never be greater than a 7. If your leadership is only a 4, then your effectiveness will be no higher than a 3. Your leadership ability—for better or for worse—always determines your effectiveness and the potential impact of your organization.

Let me give you a picture of what I mean. Let's say that when it comes to success, you're an eight (on a scale from one to ten). That's pretty good. I think it would be safe to say that the McDonald brothers were in that range. But let's also say that your leadership ability is only a one. Your level of effectiveness would look like this:

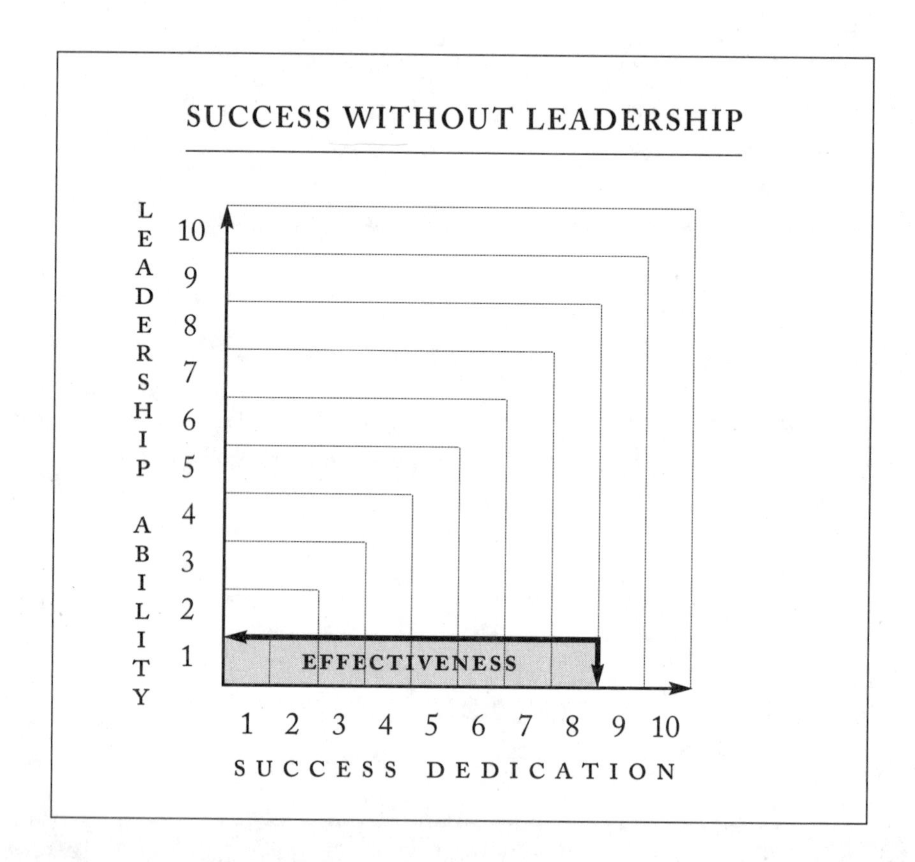

To increase your level of effectiveness, you have a couple of choices. You could work very hard to increase your dedication to success and excellence—to work toward becoming a ten. Now, it's possible that you could make it to that level, though the Law of Diminishing Returns says that the effort it would take to increase those last two points might take more energy than it did to achieve the first eight. If you really killed yourself, you might increase your success by 25 percent.

But you have another option. Let's say that instead you work hard to increase your level of leadership. Over the course of time, you develop yourself as a leader, and eventually your leadership ability becomes, say, a six. Visually, the results would look like this:

By raising your leadership ability—without increasing your success dedication at all—you can increase your original effectiveness by 500 percent! If you were to raise your leadership to eight, where it matched your success dedication, you would increase your effectiveness by 700 percent! Leadership has a multiplying effect.

EVALUATE

Rate your own leadership by placing the number 1, 2, or 3 next to each of the following statements: 1 = Never 2 = Sometimes 3 = Always

_______ 1. There is ample evidence that my leadership skills produce positive and lasting results on a consistent basis.

_______ 2. The organization's leadership asks me to do things that I have the confidence to accomplish.

_______ 3. I can answer with certainty when asked about the team's or organization's vision and direction.

_______ 4. My organization or team is growing and reaching new heights.

_______ 5. I know my productive strengths as a leader, and the leaders closest to me consistently affirm these strengths.

_______ 6. I know my weaknesses as a leader, and the leaders closest to me consistently confirm that these are weaknesses.

_______ 7. People outside of my organization offer me opportunities for leadership responsibility.

_______ 8. My mind is full of new ideas of how to strengthen and grow the team I lead.

_______ 9. I am aware of the areas where I need to improve and grow as a leader, and I have written a simple plan to strengthen these areas.

_______ 10. The leaders closest to me in the organization have confidence in my leadership ability.

_______ 11. I generally prefer influencing people over managing tasks.

_______ 12. I identify and write down the top two or three things that prevent me from becoming a better leader so I can work on these areas.

_______ 13. I have a track record of success when it comes to leadership.

_______ 14. I can work well in fluid and ambiguous situations.

_______ 15. My leadership bias and personal preference is more toward risk and uncertainty over security and stability.

_______ 16. I have an inner sense that my leadership will bring about significant change.

_______ 17. I think that I have yet to reach the "cap" of my abilities as a leader.

_______ 18. When I discover "lids" to my leadership, I am consistently able, with some time, to break through them.

_______ 19. I am completely confident that one of my gifts is leadership.

_______ 20. My leadership is affirmed by the people I lead through their commitment to the mission of organization.

_______ **Total**

50 – 60 This is an area of strength. Continue growing as a leader but also spend time helping others to develop in this area.

40 – 49 This area may not be hurting you as a leader, but it isn't helping you much either. To strengthen your leadership, develop yourself in this area.

20 – 39 This is an area of weakness in your leadership. Until you grow in this area, your leadership effectiveness will be negatively impacted.

DISCUSS

Answer the following questions and discuss your answers when you meet with your mentoring group.

1. *How effective will a person be if he increases his leadership but not his work ethic (dedication to success)?*

2. *Do you agree with the author's assessment that increasing your leadership is one of the best ways to increase your level of effectiveness? Explain.*

3. *What criteria can be used to determine a person's leadership ability? What are some clear signs of leadership strengths and weaknesses?*

4. *How long does it take you to determine a person's leadership "lid" once that person has been put in charge of a team?*

5. *Describe signs indicating that a leader has hit his or her lid?*

6. *Describe a situation in which your leadership lid negatively affected a project or task.*

7. *On a scale of 1 to 10, how would you describe your leadership? Would your spouse or colleagues agree with your assessment?*

8. *Up to now, how dedicated have you been to developing yourself as a leader? How will you increase that dedication?*

TAKE ACTION

Interview someone whom you consider to have a high leadership lid. Ideally this would be the person you listed in the OBSERVE section for: *Whom do you know whose leadership lid seems unlimited?* Ask that person the following questions:

1. *When did you first see yourself as a leader?*

2. *What are some of the greatest challenges you've faced as a leader?*

3. *What has contributed to your growth as a leader?*

4. *What are you currently doing to grow as a leader?*

5. *What is the best piece of advice that you would have for someone who aspires to be an effective leader?*

2

THE LAW OF INFLUENCE

The True Measure of Leadership Is Influence—Nothing More, Nothing Less

If you don't have influence, you will *never* be able to lead others. As Harry A. Overstreet said, "The very essence of all power to influence lies in getting the other person to participate." If no one is following you, you're not a leader. The *Law of Influence* is about obtaining followers, which makes it the basis for leadership.

READ

In late summer of 1997, people were jolted by two events that occurred less than a week apart: The deaths of Princess Diana and Mother Teresa. On the surface these two women could not have been more different. One was a tall, young, glamorous princess from England who circulated in the highest society. The other, a Nobel Peace Prize recipient, was a small, elderly Catholic nun born in Albania, who served the poorest of the poor in Calcutta, India.

What's incredible is that the impact they had made was remarkably similar. In a 1996 poll published by the London *Daily Mail*, Princess Diana and Mother Teresa were voted in first and second places as the world's two most caring people. That's something that doesn't happen unless you have a lot of influence.

How did someone like Diana come to be regarded in the same way as Mother Teresa? The answer is that she demonstrated the power of the *Law of Influence.*

In 1981 Diana became the most talked-about person on the globe when she married Prince Charles of England. Nearly 1 billion people watched Diana's wedding ceremony televised from St. Paul's Cathedral. And since that day, it seemed people never could get enough news about her. People were intrigued with Diana, a commoner who had once been a kindergarten teacher. At first she seemed painfully shy and totally overwhelmed by all the attention she and her new husband were receiving. Early in their marriage, it was said that Diana wasn't very happy performing the duties expected of her as a royal princess. However, in time she adjusted to her new role. As she started traveling and representing the royal family around the world at various functions, she quickly made it her goal to serve others and raise funds for numerous charitable causes. And during the process, she started to build many important relationships—with politicians, organizers of humanitarian causes, entertainers, and heads of state. At first she was simply a spokesperson and catalyst for fund-raising, but as time went by, her influence increased—and so did her ability to make things happen.

Diana started rallying people to causes such as AIDS research, leprosy patient care, and the banning of land mines. In fact, she was quite influential in bringing that last issue to the attention of the world's leaders. On a visit to the United States just months before her death, she met with the Clinton Administration to convince them to support the Oslo conference banning the devices. And a few weeks later, they made changes in their position. Patrick Fuller of the British Red Cross said, "The attention she drew to the issue influenced Clinton. She put the issue on the world agenda, there's no doubt about that."

In the beginning Diana's title had merely given her a platform to address others, but she soon became a person of influence in her own right. In 1996 when she was divorced from Prince Charles, she lost her title, but it didn't at all diminish the impact she was able to make on others. Instead, her influence continued to increase while that of her former husband and in-laws declined—despite their royal titles and position. Why? Diana instinctively understood the *Law of Influence.*

Ironically, even in death Diana continued to influence others. When her funeral was broadcast on television and BBC Radio, it was translated into forty-four languages. NBC estimated that the total audience numbered as many as 2.5 billion people—more than twice the number of people who watched her wedding.

Princess Diana has been characterized in many ways. Surprisingly, one word that I've never heard used to describe her is "leader." Yet that's what she was. Ultimately, she didn't make an impact because she once had a title. She made things happen because she was an influencer, and leadership is influence—nothing more, nothing less.

OBSERVE

People have many misconceptions about leadership. When they hear that someone has an impressive title or an assigned leadership position, they assume that he or she is a leader. *Sometimes* that's true. But titles don't have much value when it comes to leading. True leadership cannot be awarded, appointed, or assigned. It has to be earned. The only thing a title can buy is a little time—either to increase your level of influence with others or to erase it.

1. *How did Diana make the transition from being a representative to a person of influence?*

2. *Why did Diana's influence sustain even after her divorce from Prince Charles?*

3. *What is the most basic factor you can use to determine if someone is a leader or not?*

4. *According to the definition "leadership is influence," who are the most prominent leaders in your industry? What influence do they have over industry trends and standards?*

5. *Within your organization, who is not formally recognized as a leader, but has influence over others?*

LEARN

There are plenty of misconceptions and myths that people embrace about leaders and leadership. Here are five common ones:

The Management Myth

A common misunderstanding is that leading and managing are one and the same. In fact up until a few years ago, books that claimed to be on leadership were often really about management. The main difference between the two is that leadership is about influencing people to follow, while management is focused on maintaining systems and processes. As former Chrysler chairman and CEO Lee Iacocca said, "Sometimes even the best manager is like the little boy with the big dog, waiting to see where the dog wants to go so that he can take him there."

The best way to test whether a person can lead rather than just manage is to ask him to create positive change. Managers can maintain direction, but they can't change it. To move people in a new direction, you need influence.

The Entrepreneur Myth

Frequently people assume that all salespeople and entrepreneurs are leaders. But that's not always the case. You may remember the old Ronco commercials that appeared on television years ago. They sold items such as the Veg-o-Matic, Pocket Fisherman, and Inside-the-Shell-Egg Scrambler. Those products were the brainchildren of an entrepreneur named Ron Popeil. Called the "salesman of the century," he has also appeared in numerous infomercials for products like spray-on relief for baldness and food dehydrating devices.

Popeil is certainly enterprising, innovative, and successful, especially if you measure him by the $300 million in sales his products have earned. But that doesn't make him a leader. People may be buying what he has to sell, but they're not following him. At best he is able to persuade people for a moment, but he holds no long-term influence with them.

The Knowledge Myth

Sir Francis Bacon said, "Knowledge is power." Most people, believing power is the essence of leadership, naturally assume that those who possess knowledge and intelligence are leaders. But that isn't automatically true. You can visit any major university and meet brilliant research scientists and philosophers whose ability to think is so high that it's off the charts, but whose ability to lead is so low that it doesn't even register on the charts. IQ doesn't necessarily equate to leadership.

The Pioneer Myth

Another common misconception is that anyone who is out in front of the crowd is a leader. But being first isn't always the same as leading. For example Sir Edmond Hillary was the first man to reach the summit of Mt. Everest. Since his historic ascent in 1953, many people have "followed" him in achieving that feat. But that doesn't make Hillary a leader. In fact he wasn't even the leader on that particular expedition. John Hunt was. And when Hillary traveled to the South Pole in 1958 as part of the Commonwealth Trans-Antarctic Expedition, he was accompanying another leader, Sir Vivian Fuchs. To be a leader, a person has to not only be out front, but also have people intentionally coming behind him, following his lead, and acting on his vision.

The Position Myth

As mentioned before, the greatest misunderstanding people have about leadership is that they think it is based on position, but it's not. As Stanley Huffty said, "It's not the position that makes the leader; it's the leader that makes the position."

Look at what happened several years ago at Cordiant, the advertising agency formerly known as Saatchi & Saatchi. In 1994, institutional investors at Saatchi & Saatchi forced the board of directors to dismiss Maurice Saatchi, the company's CEO. What was the result? Several executives followed him out. So did many of the company's largest accounts, including British Airways and Mars, the candy maker. Saatchi's influence was so great that his departure caused the company's stock to fall immediately from $8 5/8 to $4 per share.[1] What happened is a result of the *Law of Influence*. Saatchi lost his title and position, but he continued to be the leader.

Although people in your organization may buy into one of these myths, when all is said and done, true leadership is influence. Leadership is the ability to obtain followers. It is the ability to influence others to follow you. Because without followers, who are you leading?

EVALUATE

Rate your own leadership by placing the number 1, 2, or 3 next to each of the following statements: 1 = Never 2 = Sometimes 3 = Always

_______ 1. People seem to want to follow me.

_______ 2. Within the context of new acquaintances, I emerge as the leader.

_______ 3. As an elementary-aged child, I was recognized as a leader.

_______ 4. My family recognizes me as a leader.

_______ 5. I find it easy to recruit people for volunteer projects.

_______ 6. It seems that people have an easy time understanding what I am trying to say.

_______ 7. I feel I am understood as a leader.

_______ 8. When I call the people of my organization or team to action, they follow my lead at least 80 percent of the time.

_______ 9. I have a great relationship with at least 80 percent the people in my organization or on my team.

_______ 10. When conflict arises between someone in the organization and myself, I confront that person one-on-one to deal with the situation.

_______ 11. Most of the key leaders in the organization agree with my leadership.

_______ 12. My team members and key leaders respect me as a leader and follow my lead enthusiastically.

_______ 13. It is easy for me to patiently listen when in a conversation, and I avoid interrupting until the other party has finished.

_______ 14. I make mistakes, but I do not make the same mistake twice.

_______ 15. I find it easy to relate to and connect with new people.

_______ 16. Concerning issues that are important to me, other leaders vote in a positive and supportive way.

_______ 17. I do not have trouble getting people to follow through with their commitments.

_______ 18. People trust me as a person and as a leader—my integrity is unquestioned.

_______ 19. I am definitely an encourager of people, so much that people migrate toward me in a crowd.

_______ 20. My influence is growing.

_______ **Total**

50 - 60 This is an area of strength. Continue growing as a leader but also spend time helping others to develop in this area.

40 - 49 This area may not be hurting you as a leader, but it isn't helping you much either. To strengthen your leadership, develop yourself in this area.

20 - 39 This is an area of weakness in your leadership. Until you grow in this area, your leadership effectiveness will be negatively impacted.

DISCUSS

Answer the following questions and discuss your answers when you meet with your mentoring group.

1. *What is the difference between management and leadership?*

2. *Do you agree with the author's assessment that leadership is influence? Explain.*

3. *What obstacles might people come up against if they have bought into one of the leadership myths?*

4. *Which of the five leadership myths do you find most often in your environment?*

5. *Why do you think people are tempted to buy into leadership myths?*

6. *Describe a situation when you were part of a team that was led by a person who was placed in charge because of his knowledge or position and not his leadership abilities.*

7. *Would you consider yourself to be a leader? Whom do you influence?*

8. *What are some positive ways you could expand your influence in your organization?*

TAKE ACTION

This week, try to influence five people: a supervisor, a colleague on your same position level, a follower in your sphere of influence, a follower outside of your sphere of influence, and a family member or close friend. It could be as simple as suggesting where to go eat, or as critical as suggesting a new direction for a project. At the end of the week, review each situation by following the instructions that follows.

Superior: ____________________

My expectations: ____________________

Result and Explanation: ____________________

Colleague - on same position level: ____________________

My expectations: ____________________

Result and Explanation: ____________________

Follower - in your area of influence: ____________________

My expectations: ____________________

Result and Explanation: ____________________

Follower - not in your sphere of influence: ____________________

My expectations: ____________________

Result and Explanation: ____________________

Family member or close friend: ______________________

My expectations: ______________________________

Result and Explanation: ______________________________

In what instances were you successful in influencing others to go along with your idea? Put a ÷ next to these occurrences.

In what instances were you unsuccessful in influencing others to go along with your idea? Put a √ next to these occurrences.

For each situation evaluate why you expected people to follow your lead. Was it because: you were in a position of authority; you were the most knowledgeable person on the subject; you were the person who came up with the original idea; you were the recognized leader? Then evaluate why you think people did or did not follow your lead.

When do you find yourself being influenced by someone else because of his or her position, knowledge, or leadership?

____

How is that similar to the way people have responded to you?

____

3

THE LAW OF PROCESS

Leadership Develops Daily, Not in a Day

Becoming a leader is a lot like investing successfully in the stock market. If your hope is to make it in a day, you're not going to be successful. *The Law of Process* shows that what matters most is what you do day by day over the long haul.

READ

There's an old saying: Champions don't become champions in the ring—they are merely recognized there. That's true. If you want to see where someone develops into a champion, look at his daily routine. As former heavyweight champ Joe Frazier said, "You can map out a fight plan or a life plan. But when the action starts, you're down to your reflexes. That's where your road work shows. If you cheated on that in the dark of the morning, you're getting found out now under the bright lights."[1] Boxing is a good analogy for leadership development because it is all about daily preparation. Even if a person has great natural talent, he's got to prepare and train to become successful.

One of this country's greatest leaders was a fan of boxing: President Theodore Roosevelt. In fact, one of his most famous quotes uses a boxing analogy. It says,

> It is not the critic who counts, not the man who points out how the strong man stumbled, or where the doer of deeds could have done them better. The credit belongs to the man who is actually in the arena; whose face is marred by dust and sweat and blood; who strives valiantly; who errs and comes short again and again; who knows the great enthusiasms, the great devotions, and spends himself in a worthy cause; who, at best, knows in the end the triumph of high achievement; and who, at the worst, if he fails, at least fails while daring greatly, so that his place shall never be with those cold and timid souls who know neither victory nor defeat.

Roosevelt, a boxer himself, was the ultimate man of action. Not only was he an effective leader, but he was the most flamboyant of all U.S. Presidents. British historian Hugh Brogan described him as "the ablest man to sit in the White House since Lincoln; the most vigorous since Jackson; the most bookish since John Quincy Adams."

Roosevelt is remembered as an outspoken man of action and proponent of the vigorous life. While in the White House, he was known for regular boxing and judo sessions, vigorous horseback rides, and long, strenuous hikes. A French ambassador who visited Roosevelt used to tell about the time that he accompanied the president on one of his walks through the woods. When the two men came to the banks of a stream that was too deep to cross by foot, Roosevelt stripped off his clothes and expected the dignitary to do the same so that they could swim to the other side. Nothing was an obstacle to Roosevelt.

At different times in his life, Roosevelt was a cowboy in the Wild West, an explorer and big-game hunter, and a rough-riding cavalry officer in the Spanish-American War. His enthusiasm and stamina seemed boundless. As the vice-presidential candidate in 1900, he gave 673 speeches and traveled 20,000 miles while campaigning for President McKinley. And years after his presidency, while preparing to deliver a speech in Milwaukee, Roosevelt was shot in the chest by a would-be assassin. With a broken rib and a bullet in his chest, Roosevelt insisted on delivering his one-hour speech before allowing himself to be taken to the hospital.

Of all the leaders this nation's ever had, Roosevelt was one of the toughest—both physically and mentally. But he didn't start that way. America's cowboy president was born in Manhattan to a prominent wealthy family. But as a child, he was puny and very sickly. He had debilitating asthma, possessed very poor eyesight, and was painfully thin. His parents weren't sure he would survive.

When he was twelve, young Roosevelt's father told him, "You have the mind, but you have not the body, and without the help of the body the mind cannot go as far as it should. You must *make* the body." And make it he did. He lived by the *Law of Process.*

Roosevelt began spending time *every day* building his body as well as his mind, and he did that for the rest of his life. He worked out with weights, hiked, ice-skated, hunted, rowed, rode horseback, and boxed. In later years Roosevelt assessed his progress, admitting that as a child he was "nervous and timid. Yet," he said, "from reading of the people I admired . . . and from knowing my father, I had a great admiration for men who were fearless and who could hold their own in the world, and I had a great desire to be like them."[2] By the time Roosevelt graduated from Harvard, he *was* like them, and he was ready to tackle the world of politics.

Roosevelt didn't become a great leader overnight, either. His road to the presidency was one of slow continual growth. As he served in various positions, ranging from New York City Police Commissioner to President of the United States, he kept learning and growing. He improved himself, and in time he became a strong leader, which is further evidence that he lived by the *Law of Process.*

Roosevelt's list of accomplishments is remarkable. Under his leadership, the United States emerged as a world power. He helped the country develop a first-class Navy. He built the Panama Canal. He negotiated peace between Russia and Japan, winning a Nobel Peace Prize in the process. And when people questioned Roosevelt's leadership—since he had become President when McKinley was assassinated—he campaigned and was reelected by the largest majority of any President.

Ever the man of action, when Roosevelt completed his term as President in 1909, he immediately traveled to Africa where he led a scientific expedition sponsored by the Smithsonian Institution. And a few years later, in 1913, he co-led a group to explore the uncharted River of Doubt in Brazil. It was a great learning adventure he said he could not pass up. "It was my last chance to be a boy," he later said. He was fifty-five years old.

On January 6, 1919, at his home in New York, Theodore Roosevelt died in his sleep. At the time, then–Vice President Marshall said, "Death had to take him sleeping, for if Roosevelt had been awake, there would have been a fight." When they removed him from his bed, they found a book under his pillow. Up to the very last, Roosevelt was still striving to learn and improve himself. He was still practicing the *Law of Process.*

If you want to be a leader, the good news is that you can do it. Everyone has the potential, but it isn't accomplished overnight. It requires perseverance. And you absolutely cannot ignore the *Law of Process.* Leadership doesn't develop in a day. It takes a lifetime.

OBSERVE

My friend Tag Short says, "The secret of our success is found in our daily agenda." If you continually invest in your leadership development, letting your "assets" compound, the inevitable result is growth over time.

1. *What are some of the challenges Roosevelt had to overcome in order to become a great leader?*

2. *What are some things Roosevelt included in his daily agenda that contributed to his leadership ability?*

3. *Roosevelt looked to his father and other leaders he read about for inspiration. Who are some of the people you look to for inspiration? Why?*

4. *Whom do you admire in your profession or area of service? Why is this person inspirational?*

5. *Whom in your profession or area of service do you think could have achieved more than he or she did? Why do you think this person settled for less? How does this person's dedication to personal growth factor into his or her level of success?*

6. *Which person from questions four and five do you identify with more? Why?*

LEARN

In a study of ninety top leaders from a variety of fields, leadership experts Warren Bennis and Burt Nanus made a discovery about the relationship between growth and leadership. They said, "It is the capacity to develop and improve their skills that distinguishes leaders from their followers." Successful leaders are learners. And that learning process is an ongoing result of self-discipline and perseverance. The goal each day must be to get a little better, to build on the previous day's progress.

THE FOUR PHASES OF LEADERSHIP GROWTH

Whether you do or don't have great natural ability for leadership, your development and progress will probably occur according to the following four phases:

Phase 1—I Don't Know What I Don't Know

Most people fail to recognize the value of leadership. They believe that leadership is only for a few—for the people at the top of the corporate ladder. They have no idea of the opportunities they're passing up when they don't learn to lead. This was driven home for me recently when a college president shared with me that only a handful of students signed up for a leadership course the school was offering. Why? Only a few thought of themselves as leaders. If they had known that leadership is influence, and that in the course of each day most individuals usually try to influence at least four other people, their desire might have been sparked to learn more about the subject. It's unfortunate, because as long as a person doesn't know what he doesn't know, he isn't going to grow.

Phase 2—I Know What I Don't Know

Usually at some point in life, we are placed in a leadership position only to look around and discover that no one is following us. That's when we realize that we need to *learn* how to lead. And of course, that's when it's possible for the process to start. As English Prime Minister Benjamin Disraeli said, "To be conscious that you are ignorant of the facts is a great step to knowledge."

That's what happened to me when I took my first leadership position in 1969. I had captained sports teams all my life and had been the student government president in college, so I already thought I was a leader. But when I tried to lead people in the real world, I found out the awful truth. That prompted me to start gathering resources and start learning from them. It also gave me another idea: I wrote to the top ten leaders in my field and offered them $100 for a half hour of their time so that I could ask them questions. (That was quite a sum for me in 1969.) For the next several years, my wife,

Margaret, and I planned every vacation around where those people lived. If a great leader in Cleveland said yes to my request, then that year we vacationed in Cleveland so that I could meet him. And it really paid off. Those men shared insights with me that I could not have learned any other way.

Phase 3—I Grow and Know . . . and It Starts to Show

When you recognize your lack of skill and begin the daily discipline of personal growth in leadership, that's when exciting things begin to happen.

A while back I was teaching a group of people in Denver, and in the crowd I noticed a really sharp nineteen-year-old named Brian. For a couple of days, I watched as he eagerly took notes, and I talked to him a few times during breaks. When I got to the part of the seminar where I teach the *Law of Process*, I asked Brian to stand up so that I could talk while everyone listened. I said, "Brian, I've been watching you here, and I'm very impressed with how hungry you are to learn and glean and grow. I want to tell you a secret that will change your life." Everyone in the whole auditorium seemed to lean forward in their seats.

"I believe that in about twenty years, you can be a *great* leader. I want to encourage you to make yourself a lifelong learner of leadership. Read books, listen to tapes regularly, and keep attending seminars. And whenever you come across a golden nugget of truth or a great quote, file it away for the future.

"It's not going to be easy," I said. "But in five years, you'll begin to see progress as your influence becomes greater. In ten years you'll develop a competence that makes your leadership highly effective. And in twenty years, when you're only thirty-nine, if you've continued to learn and grow, others will likely start asking you to teach them about leadership. And some will be amazed. They'll look at each other and say, 'How did he suddenly get wise?'

"Brian, you can be a great leader, but it won't happen in a day. Start paying the price now."

What's true for Brian is also true for you. Start developing your leadership today, and someday you will experience the effects of the *Law of Process*.

Phase 4—I Simply Go Because of What I Know

When you're in Phase three, you can be pretty effective as a leader, but you have to think about every move you make. However, when you get to Phase four, your ability to lead becomes almost automatic, reflexive. And that's when the payoff is larger than life. But the only way to get there is to obey the *Law of Process* and pay the price.

EVALUATE

Rate your own leadership by placing the number 1, 2, or 3 next to each of the following statements: 1 = Never 2 = Sometimes 3 = Always

_______ 1. I have maintained an intentional plan for growth as a leader over a long period of time.

_______ 2. I think through issues of timing when it comes to leading the people on my team.

_______ 3. I will delay a "right" decision if my team is not ready to respond to it.

_______ 4. I think through and write down the necessary steps to get my team ready for a major project.

_______ 5. My timing is good.

_______ 6. I am aware of and can name the key events or "defining moments" of my organization.

_______ 7. I am working to be a better leader.

_______ 8. I take the time to think through and write down what is needed to move my team or the organization from point A to point B.

_______ 9. I read good books on leadership and apply what I read.

_______ 10. I listen to good tapes on leadership and apply what I hear to my own leadership practices.

_______ 11. I am more focused on the "journey" than the destination.

_______ 12. I am willing to move more slowly if it means building a stronger team or organization.

_______ 13. I am aware of my specific good daily habits as a leader and see how they help me grow as a leader.

_______ 14. I am aware of the bad daily habits that hurt my leadership and prevent me from becoming a better leader. I have determined to break these habits.

_______ 15. Even when I have a good idea, I will run it by someone else before implementing it.

_______ 16. When I feel strongly about something, I still try to receive a "buy-in" from other leaders or people on my team.

_______ 17. I allow others to question my ideas without getting angry.

_______ 18. There is a definite sense of forward momentum in my life as a leader.

_______ 19. I have a small group of people to whom I am accountable as a leader on a personal level.

_______ 20. I have several relationships with people who stretch me and encourage me in my growth as a leader.

_______ **Total**

50 - 60 This is an area of strength. Continue growing as a leader but also spend time helping others to develop in this area.

40 - 49 This area may not be hurting you as a leader, but it isn't helping you much either. To strengthen your leadership, develop yourself in this area.

20 - 39 This is an area of weakness in your leadership. Until you grow in this area, your leadership effectiveness will be negatively impacted.

DISCUSS

Answer the following questions and discuss your answers when you meet with your mentoring group.

1. *According to the Law of Process, what must you be committed to in order to become a successful leader?*

2. *Do you agree with the author that leadership is a process? Why or why not?*

3. *Is leadership only for a few people? Why?*

4. *What steps do you see the other leaders in your organization taking in order to become better leaders?*

5. *A year ago, which of the Four Phases would you have placed yourself in? Why? How about today?*

6. *In the last year what has contributed the most to your growth as a leader?*

7. *What learning opportunities are available to you through your work, volunteer training, church, or other affiliations?*

8. *How will you commit to learning in order to become a better leader? What resources will you subscribe to or buy? What conferences or training classes will you attend this year?*

TAKE ACTION

While it's true that some people are born with greater natural gifts than others, the ability to lead is really a collection of skills, nearly all of which can be learned and improved. But that process doesn't happen overnight. Leadership is complicated. It has so many facets: respect, experience, emotional strength, people skills, discipline, vision, momentum, timing—the list goes on. As you can see, many of the factors that come into play in leadership are intangible. That's why leaders require so much seasoning to be effective.

This week, research or interview the person you admire as a leader in your profession or area of service. Answer the following questions of that person.

1. *What made you decide to enter the field in which you are successful?*

____
____
____

2. *Who were some of your mentors?*

____
____
____

3. *What five books have made the greatest impact on your leadership?*

____
____
____
____
____
____

4. *What daily learning or self-improvement habits do you have?*

Ask yourself:

5. *What are the three most valuable things I have learned from this person's life, which I will apply to my own leadership growth?*

   1.

   2.

   3.

6. *Read all five of the books recommended to you.*

4

THE LAW OF NAVIGATION

Anyone Can Steer the Ship, But It Takes a Leader to Chart the Course

Leroy Eims, author of *Be the Leader You Were Meant to Be*, writes, "A leader is one who sees more than others see, who sees farther than others see, and who sees before others do." In order to be a successful leader, you must learn the importance of The *Law of Navigation* and be willing to navigate the course for your followers.

READ

In 1911, two groups of explorers set off on an incredible journey. Though they used different strategies and routes, the leaders who headed the teams had the same goal: to be the first in history ever to reach the South Pole. Their stories are a life-and-death illustration of the *Law of Navigation*.

One of the groups was led by Norwegian explorer Roald Amundsen. Ironically, Amundsen had not originally intended to go to Antarctica. His desire was to be the first man to reach the *North* Pole. But when he discovered that Robert Peary had beaten him there, Amundsen changed his goal and headed toward the other end of the earth. North or south—he knew his planning would pay off.

Before he and his team ever set off, Amundsen had planned the trip painstakingly. He studied the methods of the Eskimos and other experienced Arctic travelers and determined that their best course of action would be to transport all their equipment and supplies by dogsled. When he assembled his team, he chose expert skiers and dog handlers. His strategy was simple. The dogs would do most of the work as the group traveled fifteen to twenty miles in a six-hour period each day. That would allow both the dogs and men plenty of time to rest each day for the following day's travel.

Amundsen's forethought and attention to detail were incredible. He located and stocked supply depots all along the route. That way they would not have to carry every bit of their supplies with them the whole trip. And he also equipped his people with the best gear possible. Amundsen had carefully considered every possible aspect of the journey, thought it through, and planned accordingly. And it paid off. The worst problem they experienced on the trip was an infected tooth that one man had to have extracted.

The other team of men was led by Robert Falcon Scott, a British naval officer who had previously done some exploring in the Antarctic area. Scott's expedition was the antithesis of Amundsen's. Instead of using dog sleds, Scott decided to use motorized sledges and ponies. Their problems began when the motors on the sledges stopped working only five days into the trip. The ponies didn't fare well either in those frigid temperatures. When they reached the foot of the Transantarctic Mountains, all of the poor animals had to be killed. As a result, the team members themselves ended up hauling the two-hundred pound sledges. It was grueling work.

Scott hadn't given enough attention to the team's other equipment either. Their clothes were so poorly designed that all the men developed frostbite. One team member required an hour every morning just to get his boots onto his swollen, gangrenous feet. And everyone became snow-blind because of the inadequate goggles Scott had supplied. On top of everything else, the team was always low on food. That was also due to Scott's poor planning. The depots of supplies Scott established were inadequately stocked, too far apart, and often poorly marked, which made them very difficult to find. And because they were continually low on fuel to melt snow, everyone became dehydrated. Making things even worse was Scott's last-minute decision to bring along a fifth man, even though they had only prepared enough supplies for four.

After covering a grueling 800 miles in ten weeks, Scott's exhausted group finally arrived at the South Pole on January 17, 1912. There they found the Norwegian flag flapping in the wind and a letter from Amundsen. The other well-led team had beaten them to their goal by more than a month!

As bad as their trip to the Pole was, that isn't the worst part of their story. The trek back was much worse. Scott and his men were starving and suffering from scurvy. But Scott, unable to navigate to the very end, was oblivious to their plight. With time running out and desperately low on food, Scott insisted that they collect 30 pounds of geological specimens to take back—more weight to be carried by the worn-out men.

Their progress became slower and slower. One member of the party sank into a stupor and died. Another, Lawrence Oates, was also in terrible shape. The former army officer, who had originally been brought along to take care of the ponies, had frostbite so severe that he had trouble going on. Because he believed he was endangering the team's survival, it's said that he purposely walked out into a blizzard to relieve the group of himself as a liability. Just before he left the tent and headed out into the storm, he said, "I am just going outside; I may be some time."

Scott and his final two team members only made it a little farther north before giving up. The return trip had already taken two months, and still they were 150 miles from their base camp. There they died. We know their story only because they spent their last hours writing in their diaries. Some of Scott's last words were these: "We shall die like gentlemen. I think this will show that the Spirit of pluck and power to endure has not passed out of our race."[1] Scott had courage, but not leadership. Because he was unable to live by the *Law of Navigation*, he and his companions died by it.

OBSERVE

Followers need leaders who are able to effectively navigate for them. When they're facing life-and-death situations, that necessity becomes painfully obvious.

At other times, even though the consequences are not as serious, the need is just as great. The truth is that just about anyone can steer the ship, but it takes a leader to chart the course.

1. *What were some of the things that Amundsen planned for that Scott overlooked?*

2. *How did Scott's lack of leadership skills affect his team?*

3. *In your organization what events or projects could have been planned better? What do you think the outcome would have been if the team had a leader who was a good navigator?*

4. *Who are the top navigators in your field? How have their leadership skills benefited their organizations?*

LEARN

Good navigators always have in mind that other people are depending on them and their ability to chart a good course. I recently read an observation by James

A. Autry in *Life and Work: A Manager's Search for Meaning* that illustrates this idea. He said that occasionally you hear about the crash of four military planes flying together in a formation. The reason for the loss of all four is this: When jet fighters fly in groups of four, one pilot—the leader—is designating where the team will fly. The other three planes fly on the leader's wing and follow him wherever he goes. Whatever moves he makes, the rest of his team will make along with him. That's true whether he soars in the clouds or smashes into a mountaintop.

Before leaders take their people on a journey, they should go through a process in order to give the trip the best chance of being a success:

Navigators Draw on Past Experience

Every past success and failure can be a source of information and wisdom—if you allow it to be. Successes teach you about yourself and what you're capable of doing with your particular gifts and talents. Failures show what kinds of wrong assumptions you've made and where your methods are flawed. If you fail to learn from your mistakes, you're going to fail again and again. That's why effective navigators start with experience. But they certainly don't end there.

Navigators Listen to What Others Have to Say

No matter how much you learn from the past, it will never tell you all you need to know for the present. That's why good navigators gather information from many sources. They get ideas from members of their leadership team. They talk to the people in their organizations to find out what's happening on the grass-roots level. And they spend time with leaders from outside of the organization who can mentor them.

Navigators Examine the Conditions Before Making Commitments

I like action, and my personality prompts me to be spontaneous. On top of that I have good intuition when it comes to leadership. But I'm also very conscious of my responsibilities as a leader. So before I make commitments that are going to impact my people, I take stock and thoroughly think things through. Good navi-gators count the cost *before* making commitments for themselves and others.

Navigators Make Sure Their Conclusions Represent Both Faith and Fact

Being able to navigate for others requires a leader to possess a positive attitude. You've got to have faith that you can take your people all the way. If you can't confidently make the trip in your mind, you're not going to be able to take it in real life. On the other hand, you also have to be able to see the facts realistically. You can't minimize obstacles or rationalize your challenges. If you don't go in with your eyes wide open, you're going to get blind-sided. As Bill Easum says, "Realistic leaders are objective enough to minimize illusions. They understand that self-deception can cost them their vision." Sometimes it's difficult balancing optimism and realism, intuition and planning, faith and fact. But that's what it takes to be effective as a navigating leader.

EVALUATE

Rate your own leadership by placing the number 1, 2, or 3 next to each of the following statements: 1 = Never 2 = Sometimes 3 = Always

_______ 1. I have a clear sense of mission—I know where my team is headed, and I can see the end results.

_______ 2. I take responsibility for the forming and shaping of my team's mission.

_______ 3. There is a definite plan of how to arrive at our desired results.

_______ 4. The strategy of how to arrive at our destination is logically mapped out on paper.

_______ 5. The leader and the organization in general are well informed of the strategy.

_______ 6. I draw on the talents and skills of others in order to implement a strategy.

_______ 7. A number of well-trained people and key leaders buy into the mission and take personal ownership of it.

_______ 8. I have a strong grasp on the amount of financial resources required to get my team to the next step and a plan of how to raise or request the money needed.

_______ 9. My sense of mission is strong, but I will not proceed ahead if I think the timing is wrong.

_______ 10. I am aware of the potential impacts of current demographic and cultural trends on our objectives.

_______ 11. Our strategy/plan is clearly thought through and comprehensive.

_______ 12. Our strategy/plan is simple and written in a step-by-step format.

_______ 13. The team I lead is flexible and resilient in their ability to respond to setbacks and needed modifications of the strategy/plan.

_______ 14. I have patience when it comes to implementation. I don't skip planned steps in order to make faster progress.

_______ 15. Even if fatigued or discouraged, I am willing to stay on course.

_______ 16. I spend more time planning than I do implementing.

_______ 17. I see the big picture clearly and have little difficulty in creating a plan to get there.

_______ 18. The plans my team and I design actually accomplish the desired objectives.

_______ 19. I consistently measure the results at the completion of a project against the written plans and goals in order to evaluate effectiveness.

_______ 20. I can consistently and accurately anticipate the number of people needed and select the right people to successfully complete a project.

_______ **Total**

50 - 60 This is an area of strength. Continue growing as a leader,but also spend time helping others to develop in this area.

40 - 49 This area may not be hurting you as a leader, but it isn't helping you much either. To strengthen your leadership, develop yourself in this area.

20 - 39 This is an area of weakness in your leadership. Until you grow in this area, your leadership effectiveness will be negatively impacted.

DISCUSS

Answer the following questions and discuss your answers when you meet with your mentoring group.

1. *What is the process you should go through in order to successfully navigate your team?*

2. *Do you agree that all four steps in the navigation process are necessary? Explain.*

3. *Which step in the navigation process do you find most difficult? Why?*

4. *How do you choose who to run your ideas by before implementing them?*

5. *Describe a situation in which you skipped one of the steps in the navigation process. What was the outcome?*

6. *How do you prepare your team for projects? In your opinion do you need to spend more time on planning? What prevents you from doing so? How can you more effectively plan to plan?*

7. *As a leader what steps will you take to ensure that your team will be well prepared to take on its next project or challenge?*

TAKE ACTION

Use the following acrostic to plan and execute an upcoming project with your team. Follow the example given.

Example Project: Company Growth

Predetermine a Course of Action
In order to grow we need a new facility.

Lay out Your Goals
Our goals are: design and build the facility, pay for it in 10 years, keep morale high in the process.

Adjust Your Priorities
Our priority is: to have a solid financial plan so the business isn't strained during building.

Notify Key Personnel
The people who need to know about the plan are: people with the most influence, key leaders, people working on the project.

Allow Time for Acceptance
We will announce the project in a 2 hour presentation to the board and follow up three days later.

Head into Action
The first step for building the new facility is zoning.

Expect Problems
A roadblock to our progress may be zoning issues.
We will plan for this roadblock by researching the zoning laws in our county.

Always Point to the Successes
We will give success updates by sending out a memo on every other Monday morning.

Daily Review Your Planning.
The project leaders will communicate each day by holding a 15-minute meeting each morning.

Your Project:____

Predetermine a Course of Action

In order to __________________ we need to ______________

____.

Lay out Your Goals

Our goals are:

____.

Adjust Your Priorities

Our priority is:

____.

Notify Key Personnel

The people who need to know about the plan are:

____.

Allow Time for Acceptance

We will announce the project by

________________________________ and we will follow up

____.

Head into Action

The first step for _______________________ is ____________

____.

Expect Problems

A roadblock to our progress may be ____________________

____.

We will plan for this roadblock by

____.

Always Point to the Successes

We will give success updates by

__________________________________ on ______________

____.

Daily Review Your Planning.

The projects leaders will communicate each day by ______

____.

5

THE LAW OF E. F. HUTTON

When the Real Leader Speaks, People Listen

You've probably heard of E. F. Hutton, the financial services company. Years ago, their motto was, "When E. F. Hutton speaks, people listen." Maybe you remember their old television commercials. The setting was typically a busy restaurant or other public place. In it, two people would be talking about financial matters, and the first person would repeat something his broker had said concerning a certain investment. The second person would say, "Well, my broker is E. F. Hutton, and E. F. Hutton says. . . ." At this point every single person in the bustling restaurant would stop dead in their tracks, turn, and listen to what the man was about to say. That's why I call this leadership truth the *Law of E. F. Hutton*. Because when the *real* leader speaks, people do listen. And once you understand and practice the *Law of E.F. Hutton*, you'll be able to determine who the real leader is and how to become a real leader.

READ

Young, inexperienced leaders often walk confidently into a room full of people only to discover that they've totally misjudged the leadership dynamics of the situation. I know that's happened to me! But when it did, it usually didn't take me very long to recognize my blunder. That was the case when I presided over my very first board meeting as a young leader. It occurred in the first church I led in rural Indiana, right after I graduated from college at age twenty-two. I hadn't been at the church for much more than a month, and I was leading a group of people whose average age was about fifty. In fact most of the people in the meeting had been at that church longer than I'd been alive.

I went into the meeting with no preconceptions, no agenda—and no clue. I figured that I was the appointed leader and just assumed everyone would follow me because of that. With all the wisdom and knowledge of my two decades of life experience, I opened the meeting and asked whether anyone had an issue he or she would like to discuss.

There was a brief pause as I looked around the table, and then a man in his sixties named Claude cleared his throat and said, "Mr. Maxwell, I've got something."

"Go right ahead, Claude" I said.

"Well," he said, "I've noticed lately that the piano seems to be out of tune when it's played in the service."

"You know, I've noticed the same thing," said one of the other board members.

"I make a motion that we spend the money to get a piano tuner to come out from Louisville and take care of it," said Claude.

"Hey, that's a great idea," everyone at the table started saying.

"I second the motion," said Benny, the board member sitting next to Claude.

"That's great," I said. "Does anybody else have anything?"

"Yep," said Claude, "I noticed the other day that there's a pane of glass in one of the Sunday-school rooms that's busted. I've got a piece a glass out at the farm that would fit that. Benny, you're a pretty good glazer. How about you put that glass in."

"Sure, Claude," said Benny. "I'd be glad to."

"Good. There's one other thing," said Claude. "This year's picnic. I was thinking maybe this time we ought to have it down by the lake. I think it would be good for the kids."

"Oh, that would be perfect. What a good idea," everyone started saying.

"Let's make it official," Benny said.

As everyone nodded agreement, we all waited to see if Claude had anything else to say.

"That's all I've got," said Claude. "Pastor, why don't you close us in prayer." And that's what I did. That was pretty much the whole content of my first board meeting. And it was also the day I realized who the real leader in that church was. I held the position, but Claude had the power. That's when I discovered the *Law of E. F. Hutton.*

The question for me after my first board meeting was how I was going to handle the situation in my church. I had several options. For example, I could have *insisted* on my right to be in charge. I've seen a lot of positional leaders do that over the years. They tell their people something like, "Hey, wait. I'm the leader. You're supposed to follow me." But that doesn't work. People might be polite to you, but they won't really follow. It's similar to something former British Prime Minister Margaret Thatcher once said: "Being in power is like being a lady. If you have to tell people you are, you aren't."

Another option would have been to try to push Claude out as the leader. But how do you think that would have turned out? He was more than twice my age, he'd lived in that area his whole life, and he was respected by everybody in the community. He was a member of that church before I got there, and everybody knew that he would be there long after I left.

I pursued a third option. By the time the next board meeting was ready to roll around, I had a list of items that I knew needed to be accomplished at the church. So about a week before we were scheduled to meet, I called Claude and asked him if I could come out to the farm and spend some time with him. As we did chores together throughout the day, he and I talked.

"Claude," I said, "You know, I've noticed that the front door on the church is cracked and peeling. It would look terrible to any new people coming to the church for the first time. Do you think we could do something about that?"

"Sure," said Claude, "that would be no problem."

I continued, "I went on down into the basement the other day. Did you know there's water down in there? Shoot, there are frogs hopping around down there, tadpoles swimming, and crawdads crawling. What do you think we ought to do?"

"Well John," Claude said, "I think we ought to have a work day and get that basement all cleaned out."

"That's a great idea," I said. "Would you bring that up at our next board meeting?"

"I sure will."

"There's another thing that's been worrying me," I continued. "Right now we've got only three rooms in the building besides the auditorium. One's being used as a storage room for a bunch of junk. The other two are for Sunday school, but one of them has an awful lot of kids and is getting pretty full."

"Don't say another word," said Claude, "we'll get that room all cleaned out."

"Oh, that would be great. Thank you, Claude."

At the next board meeting, when I called for new business, Claude said, "You know, I think it's about time for us to have a work day around here."

"That's a great idea," everyone around the table started saying.

"We'll have it a week from Saturday," said Claude. "I'll bring my truck, and, Benny, you bring yours too. We're going to do some painting, clean out that basement, and get the junk out of that storage room. We need it for a new Sunday-school class." Then he turned to one of the board members and said, "And Sister Maxine, you're going to teach it."

"I second that," said Benny, and that was it.

From then on, if I wanted to accomplish anything at that church, I just went out to the farm and did chores with Claude. I could always count on him to bring those things before the people, and whenever Claude spoke, people listened.

OBSERVE

If you see a disparity between who's leading the meeting and who's leading the people, then the person running the meeting is not the real leader.

1. *Why was Claude the real leader?*

2. *How did the author react to not being the real leader?*

3. *What did the author do so that his ideas and suggestions would be heard and enacted in the board meetings?*

4. *From your profession or area of service, give an example of a leader who was not the real leader. How did he or she react to the situation? What was the outcome?*

5. *Who are the "Claudes" or "Claudines" in your organization?*

LEARN

Once you learn the *Law of E. F. Hutton*, you'll never have trouble figuring out who the real leader is in just about any situation. For example, go to a meeting with a group of people you've never met before and watch them for five minutes. You'll know who the leader is. When somebody asks a question, who does everyone watch? Who do they wait to hear speak? The person they look to is the real leader.

Try it. The next time you're in a meeting, look around you. See if you notice a difference between these two kinds of leaders:

POSITION LEADERS	REAL LEADERS
Speak First	Speak Later
Need the Influence of the Real Leader to Get Things Done	Need Only Their Own Influence to Get Things Done
Influence Only the Other Position Leaders	Influence Everyone in the Room

If you can see a disparity between who's leading the *meeting* and who's leading the *people*, then the person running the meeting is not the real leader.

How do the real leaders *become* the real leaders within a group of people? First you must understand that leadership doesn't develop in just a day, and neither does a person's recognition as a leader. Over the course of time, seven key areas reveal themselves in a leader's life that cause him or her to step forward as a leader:

1. Character—Who They Are

True leadership always begins with the inner person. That's why someone like Billy Graham is able to draw more and more followers to him as time goes by. People can sense the depth of his character.

2. Relationships—Who They Know

You're only a leader if you have followers, and that always requires the development of relationships—the deeper the relationships, the stronger the potential for leadership. Each time I entered a new leadership position, the first thing I did was start building relationships. Build enough of the right kinds of relationships with the right people, and you can become the real leader in an organization.

3. Knowledge—What They Know

Information is vital to a leader. You have to have a grasp of the facts, an understanding of the factors involved, and a vision for the future. Knowledge alone won't make someone a leader, but without it, he or she cannot become one. I always spent a lot of time doing homework before I tried to take the lead in an organization.

4. Intuition—What They Feel

Leadership requires more than just a command of data. It demands an ability to deal with numerous intangibles.

5. Experience—Where They've Been

The greater the challenges you've faced in the past, the more likely followers are to give you a chance. Experience doesn't guarantee credibility, but it encourages people to give you a chance to prove that you are capable.

6. Past Success—What They've Done

Nothing speaks to followers like a good track record. When I went to my first church, I had no track record. I couldn't point back to past successes to help people believe in me. But by the time I went to my second church, I had a few. Every time I extended myself, took a risk, and succeeded, it gave followers another reason to trust my leadership ability—and to listen to what I had to say.

7. Ability—What They Can Do

The bottom line for followers is what a leader is capable of. Ultimately, that's the reason people will listen to you—and acknowledge you as their leader. As soon as they no longer believe you can deliver, they will stop listening.

EVALUATE

Rate your own leadership by placing the number 1, 2, or 3 next to each of the following statements: 1 = Never 2 = Sometimes 3 = Always

_______ 1. I have something of value and substance to say when I speak in a meeting.

_______ 2. I can easily get the attention of people in a meeting when I am trying to speak.

_______ 3. In a group discussion people will usually ask me what I think before the discussion is over.

_______ 4. When I speak in small or large groups, people seem very engaged with what I have to say.

_______ 5. After I speak, I have no regrets about what I said and how I said it.

_______ 6. When talking with others, people ask me questions and seem to want to know my opinion.

_______ 7. When my thoughts are different than the current direction of a discussion, people often migrate to my way of thinking.

_______ 8. I genuinely care about what others think and therefore intentionally practice good listening.

_______ 9. I speak with confidence and clarity because I know what I want and how to get there.

_______ 10. When I'm holding meetings over a number of weeks, people consistently show up.

_______ 11. In a one-on-one conversation when I confront someone of obvious wrongdoing, he or she generally responds positively to what I am saying.

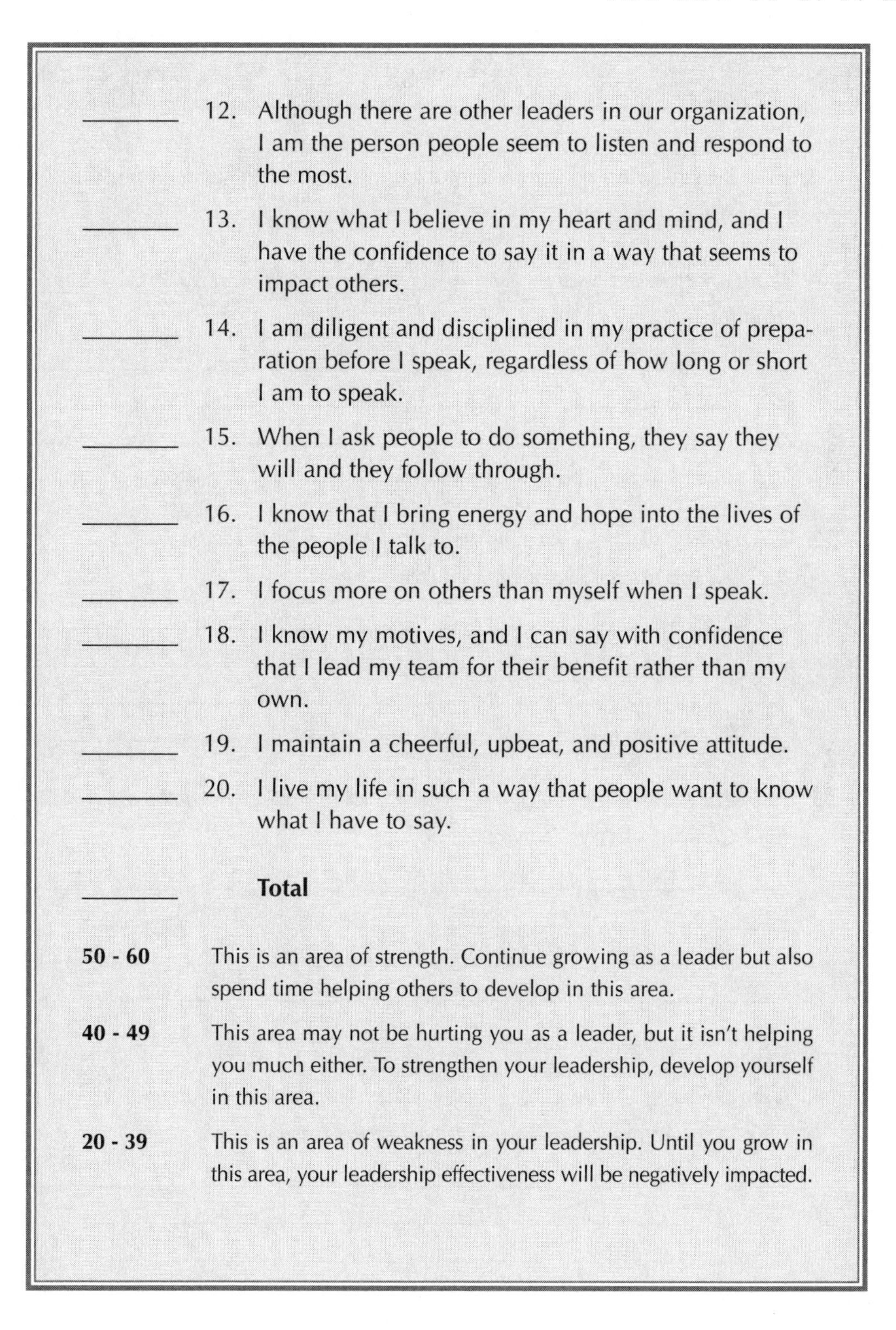

_______ 12. Although there are other leaders in our organization, I am the person people seem to listen and respond to the most.

_______ 13. I know what I believe in my heart and mind, and I have the confidence to say it in a way that seems to impact others.

_______ 14. I am diligent and disciplined in my practice of preparation before I speak, regardless of how long or short I am to speak.

_______ 15. When I ask people to do something, they say they will and they follow through.

_______ 16. I know that I bring energy and hope into the lives of the people I talk to.

_______ 17. I focus more on others than myself when I speak.

_______ 18. I know my motives, and I can say with confidence that I lead my team for their benefit rather than my own.

_______ 19. I maintain a cheerful, upbeat, and positive attitude.

_______ 20. I live my life in such a way that people want to know what I have to say.

_______ **Total**

50 - 60 This is an area of strength. Continue growing as a leader but also spend time helping others to develop in this area.

40 - 49 This area may not be hurting you as a leader, but it isn't helping you much either. To strengthen your leadership, develop yourself in this area.

20 - 39 This is an area of weakness in your leadership. Until you grow in this area, your leadership effectiveness will be negatively impacted.

DISCUSS

Answer the following questions and discuss your answers when you meet with your mentoring group.

1. *What are some of the ways you can determine who the real leader is in any situation?*

2. *What should you do if you find that although you have the leadership position, you are not the recognized (real) leader?*

3. *From the reading section, do you think the author approached the situation with Claude correctly? Explain.*

4. *Give an example of how the seven key areas of a leader's life determined who the real leader was for a group you participated in.*

5. *In your organization, who has strength in all seven key areas? How do you react to this person? How do others react to this person?*

6. *From the seven key areas of a leader's life, which is your strongest area? Why?*

7. *How can you work on the key areas that you don't feel confident in?*

TAKE ACTION

The *Law of E. F. Hutton* reveals itself in just about every kind of situation. I recently read a story about former NBA player Larry Bird that illustrates it well. During the final seconds of an especially tense game, Boston Celtics Coach K. C. Jones called a time-out. As he gathered the players together at courtside, he diagramed a play, only to have Bird say, "Get the ball out to me and get everyone out of my way."

Jones responded, "I'm the coach, and I'll call the plays!" Then he turned to the other players and said, "Get the ball to Larry and get out of his way." It just shows that when the real leader speaks, people listen.

This week go with your mentoring group to watch a basketball, football, hockey or soccer game. Determine who the real leader of the team is by asking the follow questions:

1. Who initiated the time outs? ________________
2. Who talked during the huddles? ________________
3. On the field, who did the other players look to? ________________
4. In the key play of the game, who had the ball? ________________
5. Who gave the pep talks and pats on the back? ________________
6. Who stayed calm during a fight or bad call? ________________
7. Whose mood affected the team? ________________
8. Who showed the most confidence on the field? ________________
9. Which player did the coach talk to the most? ________________
10. In the postgame interview, who mentioned teammates? ________________

After the game, discuss your observations.

6

THE LAW OF SOLID GROUND

Trust Is the Foundation of Leadership

Your good character builds trust among your followers. But if you break trust, you forfeit your ability to lead. The *Law of Solid Ground* explains all of this.

READ

My friend Bill Hybels teaches a conference with me four times a year called Leading and Communicating to Change Lives. During the 1997 conference season, Bill conducted a session titled "Lessons from a Leadership Nightmare." In it, he shared observations and insights on some of the leadership mistakes made by Robert McNamara and the Johnson administration during the Vietnam War such as: the administration's inability to prioritize multiple challenges, their acceptance of faulty assumptions, and Johnson's failure to face serious staff conflicts. But in my opinion, the greatest insight Bill shared during that talk concerned the failure of American leaders, including McNamara, to face and publicly admit the terrible mistakes they had made concerning the war in Vietnam. Their actions broke trust with the American people, and because of that, they violated the *Law of Solid Ground*. The United States has been suffering from its repercussions ever since.

Vietnam was already at war when President Kennedy and Robert McNamara, his Secretary of Defense, took office in January of 1961. The Vietnam region had been a battleground for decades, and the United States got involved in the mid 1950s when President Eisenhower sent a small number of U.S. troops to Vietnam as advisors. When Kennedy took office, he continued Eisenhower's policy. It was always his intention to let the South Vietnamese fight and win their own war, but over time, the U.S. became increasingly involved. Before the war was over, over half a million American troops would be sent to Southeast Asia.

If you remember those war years, you may be surprised to know that American support for the war was very strong even as the number of troops being sent overseas rapidly increased and the casualties mounted. By 1966 over 200,000 Americans had been sent to Vietnam, yet two-thirds of all Americans surveyed by Louis Harris believed that Vietnam was the place where the U.S. should "stand and fight communism." And most people expressed the belief that the U.S. should stay until the fight was finished.

But support did not continue for long. The Vietnam War was being handled very badly. On top of that our leaders continued the war even after they realized that we could not win it. But the worst mistake of all was that McNamara and President Johnson weren't honest with the American people about it. That broke the *Law of Solid Ground*, and it ultimately destroyed the administration's leadership.

In his book *In Retrospect*, McNamara recounts that he repeatedly minimized American losses and told only half-truths about the war. For example he says, "Upon my return to Washington [from Saigon] on December 21 [1963], I was less than candid when I reported to the press . . . I said, 'We observed the results of a very substantial increase in Vietcong activity' (true); but I then added, 'We reviewed the plans of the South Vietnamese, and we have every reason to believe they will be successful' (an overstatement at best)."

For a while, nobody questioned McNamara's statements, because there was no reason to mistrust the country's leadership. But in time, people began to recognize that his words and the facts weren't matching up. And that's when the American public began to lose faith. Years later, McNamara admitted his failure. He said, "We of the Kennedy and Johnson administrations who participated in the decisions on Vietnam acted according to what we thought were the principles and traditions of this nation. We made our decisions in light of those values. Yet we were wrong, terribly wrong."[1]

Many would argue that McNamara's admission came thirty years and 58,000 lives too late. The cost of Vietnam was high, and not just in human lives. As the American people's trust in its leaders eroded, so did their willingness to follow them. Protests led to open rebellion and to society-wide turmoil. The era that had begun with the hope and idealism characterized by John F. Kennedy ultimately ended with the mistrust and cynicism associated with Richard Nixon.

Whenever a leader breaks the *Law of Solid Ground*, he pays a price in his leadership. McNamara and President Johnson lost the trust of the American people and their ability to lead suffered as a result. Eventually, McNamara resigned as Secretary of Defense. Johnson, the consummate politician, recognized his weakened position, and didn't even run for reelection. But the repercussions of broken trust didn't end there. The American people's distrust for politicians has continued to this day, and it is still growing.

No leader can break trust with his people and expect to keep influencing them. Trust is the foundation of leadership. Violate the *Law of Solid Ground*, and you're through as a leader.

OBSERVE

Former PepsiCo Chairman and CEO Craig Weatherup acknowledges, "People will tolerate honest mistakes, but if you violate their trust you will find it very difficult to ever regain their confidence. That is one reason that you need to treat trust as your most precious asset. You may fool your boss, but you can never fool your colleagues or subordinates."

1. *How did Robert McNamara violate the trust of the American people?*

2. *How did McNamara and Johnson's actions reflect on the rest of the American government?*

3. *Give an example of a time when a leader violated your trust. What was your reaction?*

4. *After your trust has been violated, how is it regained?*

5. *Can you think of instances in which you have violated followers' trust? If so, how will you work to restore it?*

LEARN

Trust is the foundation of leadership. To build trust, a leader must exemplify three qualities: competence, connection, and character.

People will forgive occasional mistakes based on ability, especially if they can see that you're still growing as a leader. Your people know when you make mistakes. The real question is whether you're going to 'fess up. If you do, you can quickly regain their trust. If you don't, their trust might be lost forever.

Your history of successes and failures is a little like earning or spending "pocket change." Each time you make a good leadership decision, it puts change into your pocket. Each time you make a poor one, you have to pay out some of your change to the people.

Every leader begins with a certain amount of change in his pocket when he starts in a new leadership position. From then on he either builds up his change or pays it out. If he makes one bad decision after another, he keeps paying out change. Then one day, after making one last bad decision, he's going to reach into his pocket and realize he's out of change. It doesn't even matter if the blunder was big or small, when you're out of change—you're out as the leader.

A leader who keeps making good decisions and keeps recording wins for the organization builds up his change. Then even if he makes a huge blunder, he can still have plenty of change left over. You must be able to determine how much change you have as a leader, how you can build relationships, and how you can be successful in order to gain more change. If you don't, you're likely to empty your own pockets.

CHARACTER COUNTS

Although people will trust someone who blunders in ability, they won't trust someone who slips in character. In that area even occasional lapses are lethal. All effective leaders know this truth.

General H. Norman Schwarzkopf says, "Leadership is a potent combination of strategy and character. But if you must be without one, be without strategy." Character and leadership credibility always go hand in hand. Anthony Harrigan, president of the U.S. Business and Industrial Council, said,

> The role of character always has been the key factor in the rise and fall of nations. And one can be sure that America is no exception to this rule of history. We won't survive as a country because we are smarter or more sophisticated but because we are—we hope—stronger inwardly. In short, character is the only effective bulwark against internal and external forces that lead to a country's disintegration or collapse.

Character makes trust possible. And trust makes leadership possible. That is the *Law of Solid Ground.*

Whenever you lead people, it's as though they are consenting to take a journey with you. How that trip is going to turn out is predicted by your character. With good character, the longer the trip is, the better it gets. But if your character is flawed, the longer the trip, the worse it will seem to them. Why? Because no one enjoys spending time with someone he doesn't trust.

CHARACTER COMMUNICATES MANY THINGS TO FOLLOWERS:

Character Communicates Consistency

Leaders without inner strength can't be counted on day after day because their ability to perform changes constantly. As NBA great Jerry West says, "You can't get too much done in life if you only work on the days when you feel good." If your people don't know what to expect from you as a leader, at some point they won't even look to you for leadership.

Character Communicates Potential

John Morley said, "No man can climb out beyond the limitations of his own character." That's especially true when it comes to leadership. Take, for instance, the case of NHL coach Mike Keenan. As of mid-1997, he had a great record of professional hockey victories: the fifth greatest number of regular-season wins, the third greatest number of playoff victories, six division titles, four NHL finals appearances, and one Stanley Cup.

Yet despite those great credentials, Keenan was unable to stay with a single team for any length of time. In only eleven seasons, he coached four different teams. And after his stint with the fourth team—the St. Louis Blues—he was unable to land a job for a long time. Why? Sports writer E. M. Swift said of Keenan, "The reluctance to hire Keenan is *easily* explicable. Everywhere he has been, he has alienated players and management."[2] His players didn't trust his motives or methods. Even the owners, who were benefiting from seeing their teams win, didn't trust him. He kept violating the *Law of Solid Ground.*

Craig Weatherup says, "You don't build trust by talking about it. You build it by achieving results, always with integrity and in a manner that shows real personal regard for the people with whom you work."[3] When a leader's character is strong, people trust him—and they trust in his ability to release their own potential. That not only gives followers hope for the future, but it also promotes a strong belief in themselves and their organization.

Character Communicates Respect

When you don't have strength within, you cannot earn respect without. And respect is absolutely essential for lasting leadership. How do leaders earn respect? By making good decisions, admitting their mistakes when they make them, and putting what's best for their followers and the organization ahead of their own personal agendas.

J. R. Miller once observed, "The only thing that walks back from the tomb with the mourners and refuses to be buried is the character of a man. This is true. What a man is survives him. It can never be buried." Your character will determine not only your leadership ability, but also your leadership legacy. Build your leadership on the *Law of Solid Ground.*

EVALUATE

Rate your own leadership by placing the number 1, 2, or 3 next to each of the following statements: 1 = Never 2 = Sometimes 3 = Always

_______ 1. I trust others even before they've shown trust in me.

_______ 2. People rarely question my sincerity.

_______ 3. I am able to develop and maintain long-term close personal relationships.

_______ 4. When I am wrong, I will admit it quickly to everyone who is involved with the situation.

_______ 5. People seem to open up easily with me and share sensitive and confidential information.

_______ 6. I am wholly and fully committed to the truth.

_______ 7. I handle money matters well.

_______ 8. People can count on me to do what I say I will do.

_______ 9. I am the same person at home as I am outside of my home.

_______ 10. I diligently seek to give more than I get in life.

_______ 11. I can ask for forgiveness, even in public situations.

_______ 12. I am consistent in my positive mood and honest behavior.

_______ 13. It is easy for me to trust others.

_______ 14. I allow others to hold me accountable, and I am honest and open with them.

_______ 15. Trust is something that I must continually earn every day through a life of integrity.

_______ 16. I recognize that even the smallest hurt or unresolved issue can affect the confidence others have in me, and I work to resolve or address the situations.

_______ 17. If I make a promise of any kind, I keep it, no exceptions.

_______ 18. The team's trust in me is based more on who I am than on the title or position I hold.

_______ 19. I do not stretch the truth, even if it may benefit my team or myself.

_______ 20. Though not perfect, I live my life to the best of my ability.

_______ **Total**

50 - 60 This is an area of strength. Continue growing as a leader but also spend time helping others to develop in this area.

40 - 49 This area may not be hurting you as a leader, but it isn't helping you much either. To strengthen your leadership, develop yourself in this area.

20 - 39 This is an area of weakness in your leadership. Until you grow in this area, your leadership effectiveness will be negatively impacted.

DISCUSS

Answer the following questions and discuss your answers when you meet with your mentoring group.

1. *Do you agree with the author that to build trust a leader must exemplify competence, connection, and character? Can you gain trust without one of these characteristics? Is there another characteristic you would add? Explain.*

2. *How effective will a leader be if he or she has lost the trust of the team?*

3. *How does character communicate consistency, potential, and respect? Give an example for each.*

4. *What is the quickest way for a person to lose your trust?*

5. *How would you handle a situation in which you worked with someone you didn't trust?*

____

____

____

6. *How do you gain and maintain the trust of others?*

____

____

____

7. *Of the three trust-building factors—competence, connection, character—which is your strength? In which are you weakest? Why?*

____

____

____

8. *How can you improve your competence, connection, or character in order to become a better leader?*

____

____

____

TAKE ACTION

When you work with others you have a number of opportunities to display your competence, connection, and character in the decisions you make and actions you take. With every decision and action, you are either gaining or losing change, building or losing trust.

Take time to evaluate your current level of trust with the team you are leading or working with now.

1. Overall, how would your people rate your competence on a scale of one to ten?

 ____

2. Have there been times when mistakes you made held the team back? If so, how do you think it has damaged people's trust in you? How can you repair it?

 ____
 ____
 ____

3. List the names of the people on your team. Next to each name, give an example of how you have made an effort to connect with this person.

Name	**Connection**
____________	____________ ____________
____________	____________ ____________
____________	____________ ____________
____________	____________ ____________
____________	____________ ____________

4. How does your level of connection affect your ability to lead or work with the people you listed? Who should you spend more time connecting with? How do you plan to do this?

____

____

____

____

5. Give yourself a grade on a scale of 1-10 (one being an area of weakness and 10 being an area of strength) on each of the following character areas:

Commitment	1	2	3	4	5	6	7	8	9	10
Courage	1	2	3	4	5	6	7	8	9	10
Honesty	1	2	3	4	5	6	7	8	9	10
Perseverance	1	2	3	4	5	6	7	8	9	10
Preparedness	1	2	3	4	5	6	7	8	9	10
Respect for others	1	2	3	4	5	6	7	8	9	10
Responsibility	1	2	3	4	5	6	7	8	9	10
Self-discipline	1	2	3	4	5	6	7	8	9	10
Teachability	1	2	3	4	5	6	7	8	9	10
Unselfishness	1	2	3	4	5	6	7	8	9	10

Out of a possible total score of 100, how did you do? ________________
Anything other than a high score indicates a need to work on character issues.

6. To better evaluate your character, talk to someone in your work environment whom you trust and who can honestly give you feedback about what areas of your character or how you express yourself you can work on.

7

THE LAW OF RESPECT

People Naturally Follow Leaders Stronger than Themselves

When people respect someone as a person, they admire her. When they respect her as a friend, they love her. When they respect her as a leader, they follow her. There are different forms and levels of respect, and if you want to influence others you need to be respected as a leader. And in order to do that, you will have to prove yourself and your abilities as stated by the *Law of Respect.* As Clarence B. Randall said, "The leader must know, must know he knows, and must be able to make it abundantly clear to those about him that he knows."

READ

If you had seen her yourself, your first reaction might not have been respect. She wasn't a very impressive-looking woman—just a little over five feet tall, in her late thirties, with dark-brown, weathered skin. She couldn't read or write. The clothes she wore were coarse and worn, although they were neat. When she smiled, people could see that her top two front teeth were missing.

She lived alone. The story was that she had abandoned her husband when she was twenty-nine. She gave him no warning. One day he woke up, and she was gone. She talked to him only once after that, years later, and she never mentioned his name again afterward.

Her employment was intermittent. Most of the time she took domestic jobs in small hotels: scrubbing floors, making up rooms, and cooking. But just about every spring and fall she would disappear from her place of employment, come back broke, and work again to scrape together what little money she could. When she was present on the job, she worked hard and seemed physically tough, but she also was known to have fits during which she would suddenly fall asleep—some coming even in the middle of a conversation. She attributed her affliction to a blow to the head she had taken during a teenage fight.

Who would respect a woman like this? The answer is the three-hundred-plus slaves who followed her to freedom out of the South—they recognized and respected her leadership. So did just about every abolitionist in New England. The year was 1857. The woman's name was Harriet Tubman.

While she was only in her thirties, Harriet Tubman came to be called "Moses" because of her ability to go into the land of captivity and bring so many of her people out of slavery's bondage. Tubman started life as a slave herself. She was born in 1820 and grew up in the farmland of Maryland. When she was thirteen, she received the blow to her head that troubled her all her life. She was in a store, and a white overseer demanded her assistance so that he could beat an escaping slave. When she refused and blocked the overseer's way, the man threw a two-pound weight that hit Tubman in the head. She nearly died, and her recovery took months.

At age twenty-four, she married John Tubman, a free black man. But when she talked to him about escaping to freedom in the North, he wouldn't hear of it. He said that if she tried to leave, he'd turn her in. So when she resolved to take her chances and go north in 1849, she did so alone, without a word to him. Her first biographer, Sarah Bradford, said that Tubman told her:

> I had reasoned this out in my mind: there was one of two things I had a *right* to, liberty or death. If I could not have one, I would have the other, for no man should take me alive. I should fight for my liberty as my strength lasted, and when the time came for me to go, the Lord would let them take me.

Tubman made her way to Philadelphia, Pennsylvania, via the Underground Railroad, a secret network of free blacks, white abolitionists, and Quakers who helped escaping slaves who were on the run. Though free herself, she vowed to return to Maryland and bring her family out. In 1850 she made her first return trip as an Underground Railroad "conductor"—someone who retrieved and guided out slaves with the assistance of sympathizers along the way.

Each summer and winter, Tubman worked as a domestic, scraping together the funds she needed to make return trips to the South. And every spring and fall, she risked her life by going south and returning with more people. She was fearless. And her leadership was unshakable. It was extremely dangerous work, and when people in her charge wavered, she was strong as steel. Tubman knew escaped slaves who returned would be beaten and tortured until they gave information about those who had helped them. So she never allowed anyone she was guiding to give up. "Dead folks tell no tales," she would tell a faint-hearted slave as she put a loaded pistol to his head. "You go on or die!"

Between 1850 and 1860, Harriet Tubman guided out more than 300 people, including many of her own family members. She made nineteen trips in all and was very proud of the fact that she never once lost a single person under her care. "I never ran my train off the track," she once said, "and I never lost a passenger." Southern whites put a $12,000 price on her head—a fortune. Southern blacks simply called her Moses. By the start of the Civil War, she had brought more people out of slavery than any other American in history—black or white, male or female.

Tubman's reputation and influence commanded respect, and not just among slaves who dreamed of gaining their freedom. Influential northerners of both races sought her out. She spoke at rallies and in homes throughout Philadelphia, Pennsylvania; Boston, Massachusetts; St. Catharines, Canada; and Auburn, New York, where she eventually settled. People of prominence sought her out, such as Senator William Seward, who later became Abraham Lincoln's Secretary of State, and outspoken abolitionist and former slave Frederick Douglas. Tubman's advice and leadership were also requested by John Brown, the famed revolutionary abolitionist. Brown always referred to the former slave as "General Tubman" and was quoted as saying she "was a better officer than most whom he had seen, and could command an army as successfully as she had led her small parties of fugitives."[1] That is the essence of the *Law of Respect.*

OBSERVE

Harriet Tubman would appear to be an unlikely candidate for leadership, because the deck was certainly stacked against her. But despite her circumstances, she became an incredible leader. The reason is simple: People naturally follow leaders stronger than themselves. Everyone who came in contact with her recognized her strong leadership ability and felt compelled to follow her. That's how the *Law of Respect* works.

1. *Why wasn't Harriet Tubman an obvious choice as a leader?*

2. *How did Harriet Tubman gain respect?*

3. *How did respect factor into her leadership abilities?*

4. *Who is the person you respect the most in your profession? Why is this person so highly respected? What has this person been able to accomplish?*

5. *Who do you most respect in your organization? Why?*

____

____

____

____

____

LEARN

People don't follow others by accident. They follow individuals whose leadership they respect. What that means is that someone who is an 8 in leadership doesn't go out and look for a 6 to follow—he naturally follows a 9 or 10. The less skilled follow the more highly skilled and gifted. Now occasionally a strong leader may choose to follow someone weaker than himself. But when that happens it's for a reason. For example, the stronger leader may do it out of respect for the person's office or past accomplishments. Or he may be following the chain of command. In general, though, followers are attracted to people who are better leaders than themselves. That is the *Law of Respect*.

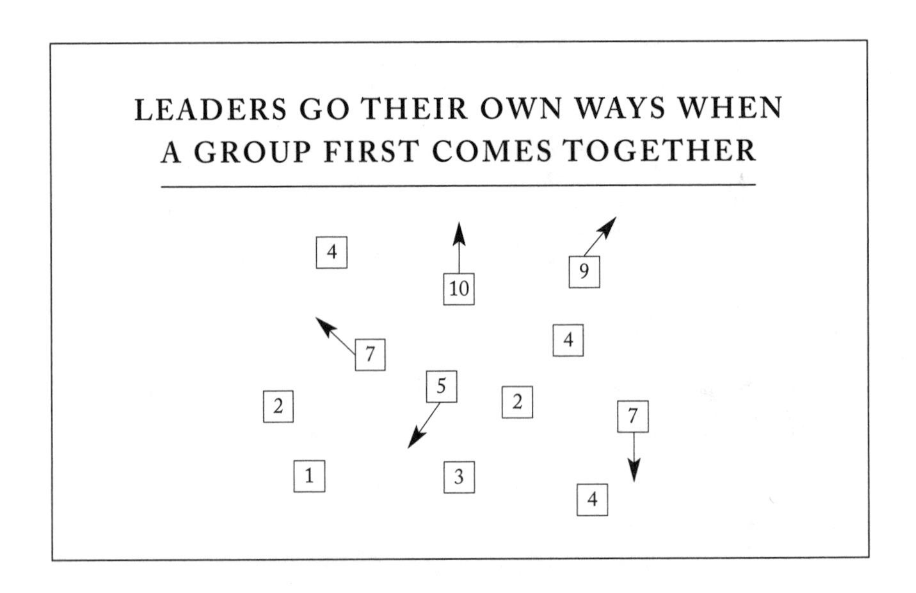

When any group of people gets together for the first time, take a look at what happens. As everyone starts interacting, the leaders in the group immediately begin taking charge. They think in terms of the direction they desire to go and who they want to take with them. At first, people may make tentative moves in several different directions, but after the people get to know one another, it doesn't take long for them to recognize who the strongest leaders are and to begin following them.

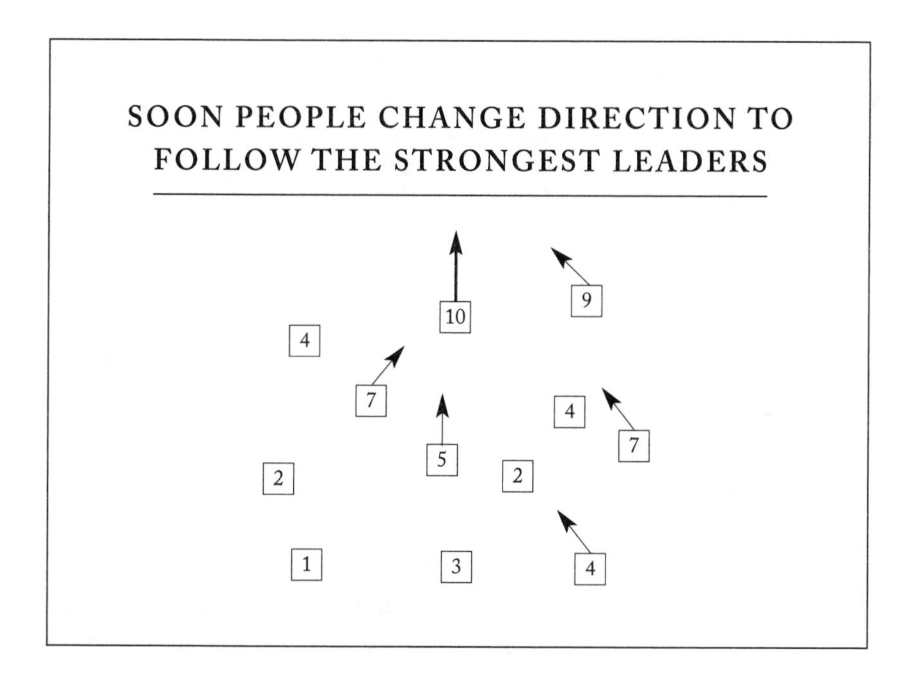

Usually the more leadership ability a person has, the more quickly he is able to recognize leadership—or its lack—in others. In time, people in the group get on board and follow the strongest leaders. Either that or they leave the group and pursue their own agenda.

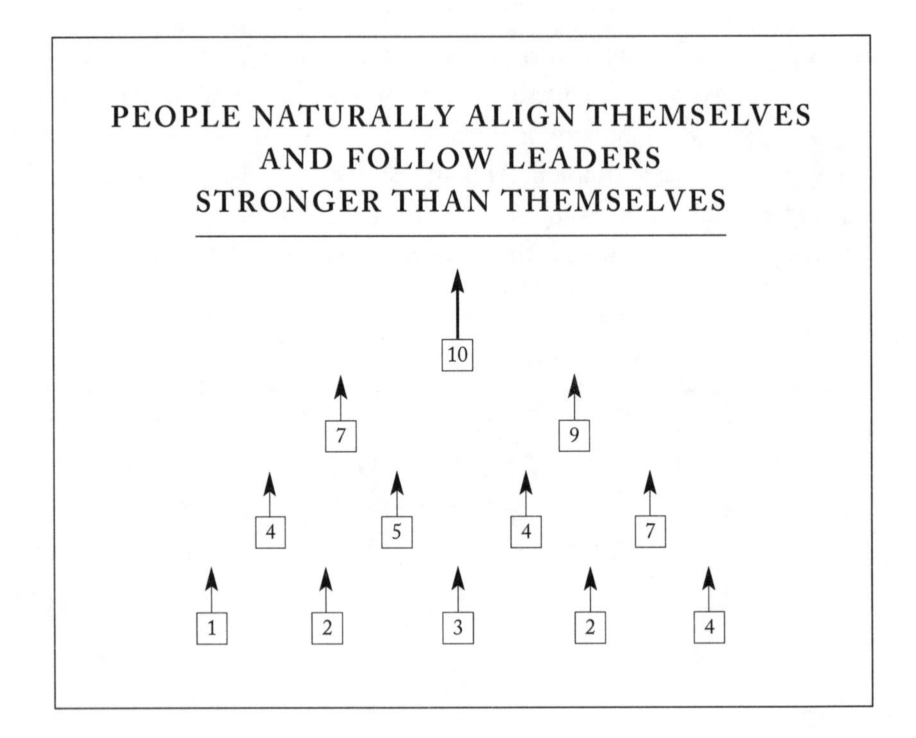

I remember hearing a story that shows how people come to follow stronger leaders. It happened back in the early 1970s when Hall-of-Fame basketball center Bill Walton joined coach John Wooden's UCLA team. As a young man, Walton wore a beard. It's been said that the coach told him his players were not allowed to have facial hair. Walton, attempting to assert his independence, said that he would not shave off his beard. Wooden's no-nonsense response was, "We'll miss you, Bill." Needless to say, Walton shaved the beard.

EVALUATE

Rate your own leadership by placing the number 1, 2, or 3 next to each of the following statements: 1 = Never 2 = Sometimes 3 = Always

_______ 1. I make things happen and get things done with positive results.

_______ 2. I will confront people when necessary.

_______ 3. The leaders in my organization know and appreciate my skills and leadership competency.

_______ 4. When I feel very strongly in favor of an issue, other people are likely to support it.

_______ 5. My family respects me as much if not more than the other people I often come in contact with.

_______ 6. As a leader, I can accomplish tasks that other leaders have not been able to accomplish.

_______ 7. The people closest to me treat me with a great deal of respect.

_______ 8. My actions are guided by my convictions.

_______ 9. I would rather make the final decision than pass the decision off to someone else, even when the decision might be hard to make.

_______ 10. I know what I want in life, and I know how to get it.

_______ 11. I am unconditionally committed to putting the needs of the people closest to me ahead of my own needs.

_______ 12. I make sacrifices based on my convictions and beliefs.

_______ 13. I am willing to stand alone even when facing tough issues.

_______ 14. I have the courage to say no.

_______ 15. I am known for working hard and possessing a strong work ethic.

_______ 16. I can admit when I am wrong.

_______ 17. I can easily recruit people to the causes I believe to be vital to the organization or community.

_______ 18. When faced with a difficult personnel issue, I have the experience and confidence to handle it.

_______ 19. I know what my specific strengths and weaknesses are as a leader.

_______ 20. I tell the truth no matter what.

_______ **Total**

50 - 60 This is an area of strength. Continue growing as a leader but also spend time helping others to develop in this area.

40 - 49 This area may not be hurting you as a leader, but it isn't helping you much either. To strengthen your leadership, develop yourself in this area.

20 - 39 This is an area of weakness in your leadership. Until you grow in this area, your leadership effectiveness will be negatively impacted.

DISCUSS

Answer the following questions and discuss your answers when you meet with your mentoring group.

1. *Under what circumstances would a strong leader follow a weaker leader?*

2. *Briefly describe the three phases that most groups go through when they first come together.*

3. *Do you agree that in most cases people choose to follow leaders who they respect? Explain.*

4. *How do you determine the strongest leader in the group?*

5. *From your own experience or observation, describe what happens when two strong leaders are placed in the same group.*

6. *Think about a current group in which you are voluntarily participating. Why is the person who is leading the group the leader? What form of respect do you have for the leader (position, friendship, admiration, leadership, past accomplishments)?*

7. *How do you react when you are placed in a group of strong leaders?*

8. *What are you doing or what will you start to do to increase your level of respect among the people you interact with often or daily?*

TAKE ACTION

Having the respect of those closest to you is priceless. I think success is having the people who know me the best, respect me the most. Respect is not always the result of having other people agree with you, and because we are all unique individuals we are not going to agree on everything. But gaining the respect of the people who know us the best—our success and failures, beliefs and convictions, strengths and weakness, character and motives—is an accomplishment.

This week gather together three of your friends for a discussion. Come up with at least five situations that you and your friends might find yourself in as a group. (Example: planning a trip, entering a business venture, experiencing a medical emergency, teaming up to play a sport, etc.) For each situation, have each person tell which person in the group they would most likely follow and why. List the situations you and your friends came up with below, and list the names of who was mentioned as the leader for each situation.

Situation	**Leader**
______________________	______________________
______________________	______________________
______________________	______________________
______________________	______________________
______________________	______________________
______________________	______________________

From this exercise, recognize that different people take the leadership position at different times depending on their skills, personality, and leadership ability.

Who was named as the leader the most? Why?

____

____

____

Who was named as the leader the fewest times? Why?

____

____

____

How often were you named as the person they would follow? What does that say about your leadership? How could you gain more of their respect?

____

____

____

8

THE LAW OF INTUITION

Leaders Evaluate Everything with a Leadership Bias

Of all the laws of leadership, the *Law of Intuition* is probably the most difficult to understand. Why? Because it depends on so much more than *just the facts*. The *Law of Intuition* is based on facts *plus* instinct and other intangible factors. And the reality is that leadership intuition is often the one thing that separates the greatest leaders from the ones who are merely good.

READ

Several years ago when I was still living in San Diego, there were three players competing on the Chargers football team for the starting quarterback's position. My friend Tim Elmore asked me who I thought would secure the job, and without hesitation, I said "Stan Humphries."

"Really?" said Tim. "I didn't think he had a chance. He's not all that big, and they say he doesn't have a strong work ethic in the weight room. He doesn't even really look like a quarterback."

"That doesn't matter," I said. "He's a better leader. Watch Stan play, and you'll see that he has the ability to read just about any situation, call the right play, and pull it off. He's the one who'll get the job." And Stan did get the job.

In fact he was so good that he was able to lead a fairly weak San Diego team to the Super Bowl in 1995.

All professional quarterbacks have great physical talent. At the pro level the differences in physical ability really aren't that great. What makes one man a third-string backup and another a Hall of Famer is intuition. The great ones can see things others can't, make changes, and move forward before others know what's happening.

I learned a lot about how quarterbacks are trained to think when I was invited to visit USC by coach Larry Smith. He asked me to come up and speak to the Trojans football team before one of their big games. While I was there, I also got to visit their offensive war room. On chalkboards covering every wall, the coaches had mapped out every possible situation their team could be in—according to down, yardage, and place on the field. And for every situation, the coaches had mapped out a specific play designed to succeed, based on their years of experience and their intuitive knowledge of the game. Together those plays constituted the approach and bias they would bring into the game in order to win it. The three USC quarterbacks had to memorize every one of those plays. And the night before the game, I watched as the coaches fired one situation after another at those three young men, requiring them to tell which play was the right one to be called.

After they were done I noticed that the offensive coordinator headed for a cot in the war room, and I said, "Aren't you going home to get some sleep?"

"No," he said. "I always spend Friday night here to make sure that *I* know all the plays too."

"Yeah, but you've got all of them written down on that sheet that you'll carry with you tomorrow on the sidelines," I said. "Why don't you just use that?"

"I can't rely on that," he answered, "there isn't time. You see, by the time the ball carrier's knee touches the ground, I have to know what play to call next. There's no time to fumble around deciding what to do." It was his job to put the coaching staff's intuition into action in an instant.

The kind of informed intuition that coaches and quarterbacks have on game day is similar to what leaders exhibit. Leaders see everything with a leadership bias, and as a result they instinctively, almost automatically, know what to do.

OBSERVE

A leader has to be able to read the situation and know instinctively what play to call. And it's this read-and-react instinct that will identify the great leaders.

1. *Why did Stan Humphries become the lead quarterback despite his size?*

2. *Define* intuition.

3. *How does the amount of time a leader has to make a decision relate to the Law of Intuition?*

4. *In your profession or area of service, how has leadership intuition accelerated the success of one organization over another?*

LEARN

Because of their intuition, leaders evaluate everything with a leadership bias. Some people are born with great leadership intuition. Others have to work hard to develop and hone it. But either way it evolves, the result is a combination of natural ability and learned skills. Together they create an informed intuition that makes leadership issues jump out at leaders. The best way to describe this bias is an ability to get a handle on intangible factors, understand them, and work with them to accomplish leadership goals.

Intuition helps leaders become readers of the numerous intangibles of leadership:

Leaders Are Readers of Their Situation

In all kinds of circumstances, they capture details that elude others. For example, when I was the senior pastor of Skyline, my church in San Diego, there were times when I was required to travel for long periods of time. Often when I returned after being gone for 10 to 14 days, I could tell something was going on. I could feel it. And usually in an hour or so of talking with staff and getting the pulse of what was going on, I'd be able to track it down.

Leaders Are Readers of Trends

Everything that happens around us does so in the context of a bigger picture. Leaders have the ability to step back from what's happening at the moment and see not only where they and their people have gone, but where they are headed in the future. It's like they can smell change in the wind.

Leaders Are Readers of Their resources

One of the major differences between achievers and leaders is how they see resources. Successful individuals think in terms of what they themselves can do. Successful leaders, on the other hand, see every situation in terms of the resources that are available: money, raw materials, technology, and most important, people. They never forget that people are their greatest asset.

Leaders Are Readers of People

President Lyndon Johnson once said that when you walk into a room, if you can't tell who's for you and who's against you, you don't belong in politics. That statement also applies to leadership. Intuitive leaders can sense what's happening among people and almost instantly know what their hopes, fears, and concerns are.

Leaders Are Readers of Themselves

Finally, good leaders develop the ability to read themselves—their strengths, skills, weaknesses, and current state of mind. They recognize the truth of what James Russell Lovell said: "No one can produce great things who is not thoroughly sincere in dealing with himself."

HOW DO YOU SEE IT?

Everyone is capable of developing a degree of leadership intuition, though we don't all start off at the same place. I've found that there are three major intuition levels that all people fit into:

1. Those Who *Naturally* See It

Some people are born with great leadership gifts. They instinctively understand people and know how to move them from point A to point B. Even when they're kids they act as leaders. Watch them on the playground and you can see everyone is following them. People with natural leadership intuition can build upon it and become world-class leaders of the highest caliber. This natural ability is often the difference between a 9 (an excellent leader) and a 10 (a world-class leader).

2. Those Who Are *Nurtured* To See It

Not everyone starts off with great instincts, but whatever abilities people have can be nurtured and developed. The ability to think like a leader is *informed* intuition. Even someone who doesn't start off as a natural leader can become an excellent one. People who don't develop the intuition they do have, are condemned to be blind-sided in their leadership for the rest of their lives.

3. Those Who Will *Never* See It

I believe nearly everyone is capable of developing leadership skills and intuition. But occasionally I run across someone who doesn't seem to have a leadership bone in his body and who has no interest in developing the skills necessary to lead. Those people will never think like anything but followers.

Leadership is really more art than science. The principles of leadership are constant, but the application changes with every leader and every situation. That's why it requires intuition. Without it, you can get blind-sided, and that's one of the worst things that can ever happen to a leader. If you want to lead for a long time, you've got to obey the *Law of Intuition*.

EVALUATE

Rate your own leadership by placing the number 1, 2, or 3 next to each of the following statements: 1 = Never 2 = Sometimes 3 = Always

_______ 1. I trust my own gut instincts as a leader.

_______ 2. My immediate impression of what to do in a certain situation is often right.

_______ 3. I have the ability to sense issues, either problems or opportunities, before they become a reality.

_______ 4. The key people around me trust and seek out my intuition as a leader.

_______ 5. My emotions do not dictate my intuition.

_______ 6. The more I learn about human nature, the better my intuition gets.

_______ 7. I seldom second-guess my leadership thoughts.

_______ 8. My intuition is more of an intentional effort than a mystical process.

_______ 9. My leadership intuition involves some very practical and intentional things like asking good questions and creative thinking.

_______ 10. The decisions I make on an intuitive basis are good decisions.

_______ 11. My first instinct and impression about a person is accurate.

_______ 12. I can defend my decisions based upon intuition with logical reasons.

_______ 13. My ability to accurately sense and assess the mood and overall morale of a group of people is very good.

_______ 14. My ability to accurately sense and assess the mood and overall morale of an individual is very good.

_______ 15. I can persuade people to buy into my leadership "hunches."

_______ 16. When a new idea is presented, I will usually know immediately if it's a good idea.

_______ 17. My leadership intuition is improving.

_______ 18. When my intuition causes me to lead against the status quo, I can still persuade the people to follow my "unconventional" direction.

_______ 19. When it comes to long-range planning, my intuition serves me well.

_______ 20. I am one of the first people in my organization to know what changes need to be made.

_______ **Total**

50 - 60 This is an area of strength. Continue growing as a leader but also spend time helping others to develop in this area.

40 - 49 This area may not be hurting you as a leader, but it isn't helping you much either. To strengthen your leadership, develop yourself in this area.

20 - 39 This is an area of weakness in your leadership. Until you grow in this area, your leadership effectiveness will be negatively impacted.

DISCUSS

Answer the following questions and discuss your answers when you meet with your mentoring group.

1. *How would you define* intuition?

2. *What creates intuition?*

3. *Do you agree with the author that intuition is not only natural but can also be developed? Explain.*

4. *Describe a situation in which leadership intuition affected your organization.*

5. *At which level of leadership intuition are you? How has your intuition affected your performance and leadership ability?*

____

____

____

6. *Which presents the biggest challenge for you: accurately reading your situation, trends, your resources, other people, or yourself? How can you improve your intuition in this area?*

____

____

____

7. *What are some resources that you will invest in to improve your leadership intuition?*

____

____

____

TAKE ACTION

How you see your world around you is determined by who you are. And while most people will just be accepting of situations, the intuitive leader looks at every situation and asks questions: Why is it this way? Why is it the popular choice? Why does it or why doesn't it work? What other ways could the situation be approached or the problem be solved? The intuitive leader observes and assesses.

Explore a leadership situation that either you or someone else is in where the decisions being made just don't seem right to you. It could be a situation in which you are the leader and everyone around you is telling you things are fine, but you still have some hesitation. Or it could be a situation in which you think another leader handled a situation incorrectly. Look at different ways the situation could be approached by answering the following questions:

1. *What is the situation?*

2. *What is the popular choice? Why?*

3. *Why does it or doesn't it work?*

4. *What is your leadership intuition telling you?*

5. *What leadership law might it be violating?*

6. *Is the job being done as well as it could be?*

7. *Is what's being done damaging relationships?*

8. *What other way could the situation be approached or the problem be solved?*

9

THE LAW OF MAGNETISM

Who You Are
Is Who You Attract

You've probably heard the saying, "Birds of a feather flock together." And maybe you've already found this to be true. When you were in school, you might have recognized that good students spent time with good students, people who only wanted to play stuck together, and so on. Well, this idea is also true when it comes to leadership. Who is on your team is seldom determined by what you want, but more by who you are. In order to build a strong team, you must understand the *Law of Magnetism.*

READ

The NFL's Dallas Cowboys had a squeaky clean image in the '60s and '70s. Tex Schramm was the president and general manager of the team, and Tom Landry was the coach. Players were men like Roger Staubach, called "Captain Comeback," a good family man with strong values similar to those of Tom Landry. Back in those days, the Cowboys were called "America's Team." They were one of the most popular groups of athletes around the country. And they were respected not only because of the talent and character of the individuals associated with the organization, but for their incredible ability to work together as a team. As they developed a winning tradition in Dallas, they continued to attract more winners.

But in the '90s the Dallas Cowboys became a very different kind of team. They changed, and their image did too. Instead of working together as a team, they sometimes appeared to be a loosely associated group of individuals who were in the game solely for their own benefit. Various players, such as wide receiver Michael Irvin, had been on the wrong side of the law. Even coach Barry Switzer found himself in trouble several times, such as when he tried to take a loaded gun through the security gate at an airport. Why had the complexion of the team changed so drastically? It's the *Law of Magnetism*. In 1989 the Cowboys' ownership changed. The new owner, Jerry Jones, is an individualist and something of a maverick. He had no qualms about going out and signing his own deals with shoe and soft drink companies despite the fact that all the NFL teams had already signed a collective endorsement contract with a competitor.

It's little wonder that the Cowboys don't enjoy the reputation they once had, even with Super Bowl victories. The Cowboys' last few coaches seem to be moving the team in the right direction. But who knows if they'll ever rise again to the level of their glory days.

OBSERVE

Al McGuire, former head basketball coach of Marquette University, once said, "A team should be an extension of the coach's personality. My teams were arrogant and obnoxious." I say that a team cannot be anything *but* an extension of their coach's personality.

1. *How and why did the Cowboys' team change from the '60s to the '90s?*

____

____

____

____

____

2. *Why would a football team's image be important to maintain?*

3. *Do you agree with the author's statement that the team is an extension of the coach's personality? Give an example that supports your answer.*

4. *Give an example of how leaders attract people like themselves from your own industry or area of service.*

LEARN

It is possible for a leader to go out and recruit people unlike him- or herself. In fact, good leaders know that one of the secrets to success is to staff their weaknesses. That way they can focus and function in their areas of strength while others take care of those important matters that would otherwise be neglected. But it's crucial to recognize that people who are different will not be naturally attracted to you. Leaders draw people who are like themselves.

You will find that the people who are drawn to you probably have more similarities than differences, especially in a few key areas. Take a look at the five following characteristics. You will probably find that you and the people who follow you share common ground in several of these key areas:

1. Attitude

Rarely have I seen positive and negative people attracted to one another. People who see life as a series of great opportunities and exciting challenges don't want to hear others talk about how bad things are all the time. I know that's true for me. I can't think of a single negative person in leadership at my organizations.

2. Generation

People also tend to attract others of roughly the same age. For instance, Kevin Small, the president of one of my companies, is a sharp, aggressive guy in his early thirties. He is married, and he and his wife had their first child last year. Can you guess what kind of people he attracts? Most of them are aggressive guys in their late twenties or early thirties that are married and starting families. Who you are is who you attract.

3. Background

One of the things Theodore Roosevelt is best remembered for is his daring charge up San Juan Hill with the Rough Riders during the Spanish-American War. Roosevelt himself recruited that all-volunteer cavalry company, and it was said to be a remarkably peculiar group of people. It was comprised primarily of two types of men: wealthy aristocrats from the northeast and cowboys from the wild west. Why? Because Roosevelt was an aristocratic-born, Harvard-educated New Yorker who turned himself into a real-life cowboy and big-game hunter in the Dakotas of the West. He was a strong and genuine leader in both of those worlds, and as a result he attracted both kinds of people.

4. Values

People are also attracted to leaders whose values are similar to their own. Think about the kinds of people who flocked to President John F. Kennedy after he was elected in 1960. He was a young idealist who wanted to change the world. And he attracted people with a similar profile. When he formed the Peace Corps and called people to service, saying, "Ask not what your country can do for you. Ask what you can do for your country," thousands of young, idealistic people stepped forward to answer the challenge.

When it comes to values, it doesn't matter whether the ones shared are positive or negative. Whatever character you possess you will likely find in the people who follow you.

5. Life Experience

Life experience is another area of attraction for people. For example, any time I speak to any new audience, I can tell within thirty seconds what kind of speaker they are used to hearing. If they regularly listen to gifted and energetic communicators, they are a sharp and responsive audience. You can see it in their faces. Their sense of expectation is high, their body language is positive, and when you get ready to speak, they've got paper and pencil ready to take notes. But if a group of people is used to a poor communicator, I find that they just kind of lay back and check out mentally.

6. Leadership Ability

Finally, the people you attract will have leadership ability similar to your own. People naturally follow leaders stronger than themselves, but you also have to factor in the *Law of Magnetism*, which states that who you are is who you attract. What that means is that if you are a seven when it comes to leadership, you are more likely to draw fives and sixes to you than twos and threes. Like attracts like. The leaders you attract will be similar in style and ability to you.

A great example of the *Law of Magnetism* can be seen among the military leaders of the Civil War. When the Southern states seceded, there were questions about which side many of the generals would fight for. Robert E. Lee was considered the best general in the nation, and he was actually offered command of the Union Army by President Lincoln. But Lee would never consider fighting against his native Virginia. He declined the offer and joined the Confederacy—and the best generals in the land followed him.

If Lee had chosen to lead an army for the Union instead, many other good generals would have followed him north. As a result, the war probably would have been much shorter. It might have lasted two years instead of five—and hundreds of thousands of lives would have been saved. It just goes to show you that the better leader you are, the better leaders you will attract. And that has an incredible impact on everything you do.

EVALUATE

Rate your own leadership by placing the number 1, 2, or 3 next to each of the following statements: 1 = Never 2 = Sometimes 3 = Always

_______ 1. The people I attract are friendly and servant-oriented.

_______ 2. As it relates to the people I attract, my strengths are an asset to the growth of my organization.

_______ 3. I attract people to myself and to my organization.

_______ 4. The people I attract help my organization to grow.

_______ 5. My general disposition is that of a positive attitude.

_______ 6. The kinds of people that I attract are the kind of people I want to attract.

_______ 7. The people I'm attracting are skilled and talented.

_______ 8. As I change and grow as a leader, I attract a higher caliber of people.

_______ 9. I tend to see opportunities and solutions as quickly as I recognize problems.

_______ 10. I have personal confidence as a leader.

_______ 11. I have a high energy level.

_______ 12. I have a good sense of humor.

_______ 13. I know what to do and when to do it.

_______ 14. I'm thrilled with the caliber of key leaders around me and often think, "I couldn't have a better team."

_______ 15. I am others-focused and intentionally invest myself in the personal growth of others.

_______ 16. I like who I am and who I attract.

_______ 17. I like who I am becoming as a leader.

_______ 18. Other leaders seem to migrate towards me.

_______ 19. The primary influencers of my organization are encouraged about the kind of leaders I'm attracting to the organization.

_______ 20. The people who migrate toward me have their acts together.

_______ **Total**

50 - 60 This is an area of strength. Continue growing as a leader but also spend time helping others to develop in this area.

40 - 49 This area may not be hurting you as a leader, but it isn't helping you much either. To strengthen your leadership, develop yourself in this area.

20 - 39 This is an area of weakness in your leadership. Until you grow in this area, your leadership effectiveness will be negatively impacted.

DISCUSS

Answer the following questions and discuss your answers when you meet with your mentoring group.

1. *Why wasn't Abraham Lincoln able to attract Robert E. Lee to the Union Army? Which common ground area did Lee's reason fall into?*

2. *Give an example of how background can attract people to certain companies.*

3. *How have the six common-ground areas played a part in the makeup and growth of your organization?*

4. *Which of the common-ground areas has the strongest draw in deciding whom you follow? Explain.*

5. *Which of the common ground areas do you find attracts the most people to you? Give an example.*

6. *How has your ability to attract others positively or negatively affected your leadership?*

7. *How can you work to become a more magnetic leader?*

TAKE ACTION

Effective leaders are always on the lookout for good people. I think each of us carries around a mental list of what kind of people we would like to have in our organization. Think about it. Do you know who you're looking for right now? What is your profile of the perfect employee? What does he or she look like? What qualities do those people possess? Do you want them to be aggressive and entrepreneurial? Are you looking for great leaders? Do you care whether they are in their 20s, 40s, or 60s? Make a list of the qualities you'd like to see in the people on your team.

My People Would Have These Qualities

1. ______________________________ ______
2. ______________________________ ______
3. ______________________________ ______
4. ______________________________ ______
5. ______________________________ ______
6. ______________________________ ______
7. ______________________________ ______
8. ______________________________ ______
9. ______________________________ ______
10. ______________________________ ______

Next to each characteristic you identified, check to see if you possess that quality yourself. For example if you wrote that you would like "great leaders" and you are an excellent leader, that's a match. Put a check by it. But if your leadership is no better than average, put an *X* and write "only average leader" next to it. If you wrote that you want people who are "entrepreneurial," and you possess that quality, put a check. Otherwise, mark it with an *X,* and so on. Now look at the whole list.

If you see a whole bunch of *X*s, then you're in trouble, because the people you described are not the type who will want to follow you. In most situations you draw people to you who possess the same qualities you do.

What can you do to possess the qualities on your list that you put an *X* next to? Who can you learn from? What resources would help you? Create a plan to improve yourself.

1. ______________________________

2. ______________________________

3. ______________________________

4. ______________________________

5. ______________________________

6. ______________________________

7. ______________________________

8. ______________________________

9. ______________________________

10. ______________________________

10

THE LAW OF CONNECTION

Leaders Touch a Heart Before They Ask for a Hand

Communication is vital to leadership. And all great communicators recognize and practice the *Law of Connection.* They know that you can't move people to action unless you first move them with emotion.

READ

Not long ago, I made a trip to San Jose, California, to see an event sponsored by their local chamber of commerce. Speaking that day was an all-star cast of communicators, people like Mark Russell who used humor so effectively, Mario Cuomo who infused passion into everything he said, the brilliant Malcolm Forbes whose insight made every subject he talked about seem brand-new, and Colin Powell whose confidence gave everyone in the audience security and hope. Every one of those communicators was strong and was able to develop an incredible rapport with the audience. But as good as they were, none was as good as my favorite. Head and shoulders above the rest stood Elizabeth Dole.

No doubt you've heard of Elizabeth Dole. She is a lawyer by trade, was a Cabinet member in the Reagan and Bush administrations, and served as the

President of the American Red Cross from 1991 to 1999. She is a marvelous communicator. Her particular gift, which she demonstrated in San Jose that day, was making me and everyone else in her audience feel as if she was really our friend. She made me glad I was there. The bottom line is that she really knows how to connect with people.

In 1996 she demonstrated that ability to the whole country when she spoke at the Republican National Convention. If you watched it on television, you know what I'm talking about. When Elizabeth Dole walked out into the audience that night, everybody there felt that she was their best friend. She was able to develop an amazing connection with them. I also felt that connection, even though I was sitting in my living room at home watching her on television. Once she was done, I would have followed her anywhere.

Also speaking at that convention was Bob Dole, Elizabeth's husband—not surprising since he was the Republican nominee for the presidential race. Anyone who watched would have observed a remarkable difference between the communication abilities of those two speakers. Where Elizabeth was warm and approachable, Bob appeared stern and distant. Throughout the campaign, he never seemed to be able to connect with the people.

Certainly there are a lot of factors that come into play in the election of a president of the United States. But not least among them is the ability of a candidate to connect with his audience. A lot has been written about the Kennedy-Nixon debates of the 1960 election. One of the reasons Kennedy succeeded was that he was able to make the television audience feel connected to him. The same kind of connection developed between Ronald Reagan and his audiences. And in the 1992 election, Bill Clinton worked extremely hard to develop a sense of connection with the American people—to do it he even appeared on the talk show *Arsenio* and played the saxophone.

I believe Bob Dole is a good man. But I also know he never connected with the people. Ironically, after the presidential race was over, he appeared on *Saturday Night Live*, a show that made fun of him during the entire campaign, implying that he was humorless and out of touch. And on the show Dole came across as relaxed, approachable, and able to make fun of himself. And he was a hit with the audience. I can't help wondering what might have happened if he had done more of that kind of thing early in the campaign.

You just can't move people to action unless you first move them with emotion. The heart comes before the head.

OBSERVE

Connecting with people isn't something that needs to just happen when a leader is communicating to groups of people. It needs to happen with individuals. The stronger the relationship and connection between individuals, the more likely the follower will want to help the leader. You develop credibility with people when you connect with them and show that you genuinely want to help them.

1. *Why is it important to connect with your team?*

2. *How did Elizabeth Dole connect with her audience?*

3. *Do you agree with the author that leaders must touch a heart before they ask for a hand? Explain or give an example.*

4. *In your profession or area of service, who has mastered the Law of Connection? How do you react when you hear this person speak?*

LEARN

A key to connecting with others is recognizing that even in a group, you have to relate to people as individuals. General Norman Schwarzkopf understood this. He said, "I have seen competent leaders who stood in front of a platoon and all they saw was a platoon. But great leaders stand in front of a platoon and see it as 44 individuals, each of whom has aspirations, each of whom wants to live, each of whom wants to do good."[1]

THE SIX KEYS TO CONNECTION

Whether you are speaking one-on-one, in a small group, or to a large audience, understanding and mastering the keys to connection will increase your effectiveness as a communicator as well as a leader.

1. Personal Authenticity

Being real is the foundation of the *Law of Connection*. To know, like, and be yourself around others is the key to being able to relate to people. You are always at your personal best when you are yourself. People cannot connect with that which is not real. Being open and candid about what you think and feel will generate a response for others. They may not always agree with you, but they will be able to connect with you.

2. Relationship

Relationship is similar to personal authenticity. Authenticity is one of the components of building a relationship, but there is more involved. First, and perhaps the most important, is honesty. Nothing will violate a relationship faster than dishonesty. Second is vulnerability. In order to connect with people you must be willing to "let them in" on your own successes and failures, ups and downs. And the third is trust. If you don't have a basic trust for others, people will be slower to trust you. And without trust the relationship will hit a wall.

3. Approachability

Instead of using power or rank, making others feel important is one of the most helpful ways to connect with them and encourage them to follow you or support your cause. One of my most cherished memories was the time I met Billy Graham at his fortieth anniversary celebration of his ministry. Standing well over six feet tall with his character of steel, one would think he would be simply overwhelming. To the contrary, he was humble, friendly, kind, and treated me as if I was the most important person in the world at that moment. He was very approachable, and this provided the entryway for us to connect.

4. Mutual Rapport

This key to connection is all about having a healthy relationship that is conducted on even ground. In most relationships, one person is more educated, better networked, more experienced, makes more money or perhaps is even more intelligent. But mutual rapport says that even if this is true and you are the person on top, never act like it is. The very thought or awareness of a superior attitude prevents connection.

5. Belief in People

People know if you believe in them. And whether the encounter is brief or long term, people usually have an inner sense about your motive. They can sense if you are there for your best interest or theirs. If you don't believe the best in people then you will never be able to see their potential. And if you can't find the potential in others, you will never be able to affectively lead them and help them excel.

6. Meaning and Depth

People connect with you at the point where they see that you will add value to their life. Small talk conveys little substance. But words of encouragement, sharing a lesson, and helping another person on their journey bring depth to a relationship and open the door for connection.

Some leaders have problems with the *Law of Connection* because they believe that connecting is the responsibility of the followers. That is especially true of positional leaders. But successful leaders who understand the *Law of Connection* are always initiators. They understand that they can't wait around for people to come to them, they must take the first step in building relationships.

EVALUATE

Rate your own leadership by placing the number 1, 2, or 3 next to each of the following statements: 1 = Never 2 = Sometimes 3 = Always

_______ 1. From the first moment I meet someone new, the conversation seems to flow easily and smoothly.

_______ 2. My natural and intentional pattern, when engaged in conversation, is to focus more on the other person than on myself.

_______ 3. I feel confident when speaking to people, even those I've just recently met.

_______ 4. When I'm talking with people I perceive to be powerful and influential, I am confident and sure of what I'm saying.

_______ 5. I remember to use people's names when speaking to them.

_______ 6. When communicating with people, both individually and with crowds, I'm open, honest and transparent.

_______ 7. People say it's easy to talk to me.

_______ 8. I relate to people more on a heart-to-heart level than on a head-to-head level.

_______ 9. It is just as easy to be open with an individual as it is to be open with a large crowd.

_______ 10. When I speak to an audience, I focus on individuals more than the crowd as a whole.

_______ 11. I am aware of when I connect with people and when I don't.

_______ 12. I experience a genuine and warm connection with people.

_______ 13. I consider my connection to the audience just as important as the content of my message.

_______ 14. When addressing an audience, I am aware of the importance of the atmosphere of my immediate surroundings.

_______ 15. It is easy and natural for me to be authentic and vulnerable in both my private and public communication.

_______ 16. I can be myself around people I don't know that well.

_______ 17. People seem to open up and share things of importance and depth about themselves with me.

_______ 18. I have trust in people.

_______ 19. I maintain consistent eye contact with those I'm talking to.

_______ 20. It is easy for me to relate to what others are feeling.

_______ **Total**

50 - 60 This is an area of strength. Continue growing as a leader but also spend time helping others to develop in this area.

40 - 49 This area may not be hurting you as a leader, but it isn't helping you much either. To strengthen your leadership, develop yourself in this area.

20 - 39 This is an area of weakness in your leadership. Until you grow in this area, your leadership effectiveness will be negatively impacted.

DISCUSS

Answer the following questions and discuss your answers when you meet with your mentoring group.

1. *How does the ability to connect with others relate to leadership?*

2. *How long does it normally take to connect with someone? Describe the signs of connection.*

3. *Which of the Six Keys to Connection do you do best? Which is an area of weakness? Why?*

4. *Are there other aspects to connection? Why do you agree or disagree with the author's list?*

5. *How have you connected with someone on your team? Did you initiate the relationship or did they?*

6. *Up to now, why did you think it was or wasn't important to connect with people in your work environment?*

7. *How can you initiate healthy work relationships?*

TAKE ACTION

When a leader has done the work to connect with his people, you can see it in the way the organization functions. Among employees there are incredible loyalty and a strong work ethic. The vision of the leader becomes the aspiration of the people, and the impact is incredible.

This week, spend time connecting with someone on your team that you don't already know very well. Find an appropriate situation that will allow you to talk to them about interests outside of work. You could ask the person to join you or a group for lunch. If that's not an option, look to see if the person has anything in their workspace that might be a conversation starter (pictures of their family, college memorabilia, collectables or souvenirs in plain sight). Make it a goal to learn three things about the person on your team. Write what you learned below.

11

THE LAW OF THE INNER CIRCLE

A Leader's Potential Is Determined by Those Closest to Him

There are no Lone Ranger leaders. Think about it: If you're alone, you're not leading anybody, are you? Even the Lone Ranger had Tonto by his side. And when you begin putting together a strong inner circle, your potential will skyrocket.

READ

In 1981, I received a marvelous offer. I was working as an executive director at Wesleyan World Headquarters when I was given the opportunity to become the leader of the largest church in the Wesleyan denomination. The name of the church was Skyline, and it was located in the San Diego, California, area.

The church had a great history. It was founded in the 1950s by a wonderful man named Orval Butcher, and he was retiring after serving there for twenty-seven years. Dr. Butcher had touched the lives of thousands of people with his leadership, and the church had a strong, nationally recognized reputation. It was a good church, but it did have one problem. It had not grown in years. After making it to a little over a thousand members, it had reached a plateau.

The first time I flew out to talk with the board, I knew that Skyline was the place I was supposed to be. I immediately called and told my wife, Margaret, that we should start packing and preparing for a move. And as soon as they offered me the job, off we went with our two kids to San Diego.

As we drove across country, I began thinking about the task ahead. I was really looking forward to the challenge of taking Skyline to a new level. After we arrived, one of the first things I did was meet with each of the staff members to assess their abilities. Almost immediately I discovered why the church had flatlined. The staff I met were good people, but they weren't strong leaders. No matter what I did with them, they would never be able to take the organization to the place we needed to go. You see, every leader's potential is determined by the people closest to him. If those people are strong, then the leader can make a huge impact. If they are weak, he can't. That is the *Law of the Inner Circle.*

The task that lay ahead of me was clear. I needed to remove the weak leaders and bring in better ones. That was the only way I would be able to turn the situation around. Mentally, I divided the people into three groups according to their ability to lead and deliver results. The first group I wanted to deal with was the bottom third, the staff who contributed least to the organization. I knew I could dismiss them right away because the impact of their departure could be nothing but positive. I immediately replaced them with the best people I could find.

I then began working on the middle third. One by one, as I found good leaders from outside the organization, I brought them in and let go the weakest of the existing staff. It took me another year to process out the old middle group. By the end of three years, I had completely cleaned house, leaving only two out of the original group on staff. And because the inner circle had gone to a new level, the organization was able to go to a new level. On the new staff even the weakest of the new people were stronger than all the old ones I had let go.

As time went by, the staff continued to grow in strength. I developed the people I had to make them better leaders. And anytime a staff member left, I searched for someone even better as a replacement. As a result, the impact on Skyline was incredible. Almost as soon as I made the initial staff changes in 1981, we started growing again. In fewer than ten years, the church became three times the size it had been when I started. And the annual budget, which had been $800,000 when I got there, grew to over $5 million a year.

The growth and success we experienced at Skyline was due to the *Law of the Inner Circle*. When we had the right staff, our potential skyrocketed. And in 1995 when I left, other leaders from around the country came looking to hire my key staff members for their own organizations. They recognized the power of the *Law of the Inner Circle* and wanted to hire the very best they could find to boost their own potential.

OBSERVE

Leadership expert Warren Bennis said, "The leader finds greatness in the group, and he or she helps the members find it in themselves."[1] Although you may not be in charge yet of the hiring and firing of the people on your team, you can look for the greatness in the group and form alliances with the stronger members. Why is it that many world records are broken at the Olympics? Because when the best are challenged by the best they perform at a higher level. The same is true in all areas of life.

1. *Why did the author's church plateau at 1,000 members?*

____

____

____

2. *What steps did the author take grow to his organization?*

____

____

____

3. *Think of someone in your profession or area of service whom you consider successful. How has this person followed The Law of the Inner Circle?*

____

____

____

____

4. *How will your potential be affected if you don't form a strong Inner Circle?*

____

____

____

LEARN

Under the best circumstances, a leader should try to raise up people for his inner circle from within his own organization. Of course, that's not always possible, as my story from Skyline shows. But you can't beat the satisfaction and rewards of bringing up men and women from the "farm team."

Hewlett-Packard manager Ned Barnholt says there are three groups of people in an organization when it comes to their response to leadership and its impact: (1) those who get it almost immediately and they're off and running with it; (2) those who are skeptical and not sure what to do with it; and (3) another third who start out negative and hope it will go away. "I used to spend most of my time with those who were the most negative," says Barnholt, "trying to convince them to change. Now I spend my time with the people in the first [group]. I'm investing in my best assets"[2] That kind of attitude pays rich dividends in the future.

There are five types of people that you should try to bring into your inner circle. All of them can add tremendous value to you and your organization:

Potential Value—Those Who Raise Up Themselves

The first ability that every leader must have is the ability to lead and motivate him- or herself. Always keep your eyes open for people with potential.

Positive Value—Those Who Raise Morale in the Organization

There is an old poem by Ella Wheeler Wilcox that my mother used to recite to me. It says:

> There are two kinds of people on earth today,
> Just two kinds of people, no more, I say.

Not the good and the bad, for 'tis well understood
That the good are half-bad and the bad are half-good.
No! The two kinds of people on earth I mean
Are the people who lift and the people who lean.

People who are able to lift up others and boost the morale in an organization are invaluable, and they are always a tremendous asset to a leader's inner circle.

Personal Value—Those Who Raise Up the Leader

A friend once told me, "It's lonely at the top, so you had better know why you're there." It's true that leaders carry a heavy load. When you're out front, you can be an easy target. But you don't have to go it alone. That's why I say, "It's lonely at the top, so you'd better take someone with you." Who could be better than someone who lifts you up, not as a yes-man, but as a solid supporter and friend. Solomon of ancient Israel said, "Just as iron sharpens iron, friends sharpen the minds of each other." Seek for your inner circle people who help you improve.

Production Value—Those Who Raise Up Others

Old radio comedian Fred Allen once said about television host Ed Sullivan, "He'll be around as long as other people have talent." Though he said it as a joke, there was a lot of wisdom in his comment. Sullivan had an eye for talent and was a master at attracting talented people to his show. Many stand-up comics and musical groups who became famous in the 1960s can trace the beginning of their success back to an appearance on the Ed Sullivan Show. For your inner circle, value people capable of raising up others.

Proven Value—Those Who Raise Up People Who Raise Up Other People

The greatest value to any leader is someone who can raise up other leaders. That produces multigenerational leadership.

Lee Iacocca says that success comes not from what you know, but from whom you know and how you present yourself to each of those people. In order to increase your potential success you must seek out those people who will be an asset to your journey as well as those you can help along the way.

EVALUATE

Rate your own leadership by placing the number 1, 2, or 3 next to each of the following statements: 1 = Never 2 = Sometimes 3 = Always

_______ 1. I can identify my inner circle.

_______ 2. My inner circle exists primarily to make my life more productive.

_______ 3. I make a diligent and consistent effort to invest as much as I can into my inner circle.

_______ 4. My inner circle is made up of people who are at all different levels of leadership.

_______ 5. I intentionally seek ways to assist my inner circle of friends, colleagues and associates to grow personally and maximize their potential.

_______ 6. My inner circle consists of people within and outside of my organization.

_______ 7. I allow at least one member of my inner circle to ask me personal and hard questions about my direction, motives, and relationships.

_______ 8. My inner circle functions well as a cohesive and effective team.

_______ 9. Various people in my inner circle come up with ideas that we implement.

_______ 10. I am part of at least one other person's inner circle of leaders, colleagues or advisors.

_______ 11. The people in my inner circle are intelligent, productive and self-starters.

_______ 12. I give my time freely to my inner circle and do not resent the time commitment involved.

_______ 13. I trust everyone in my inner circle 100 percent.

_______ 14. The people in my inner circle are honest, industrious, and add value to my life and those around me.

_______ 15. My inner circle is more mission-minded than social or political.

_______ 16. I find great joy in rewarding my inner circle for their accomplishments.

_______ 17. My inner circle will protect me and support me, but never in a way that violates moral integrity.

_______ 18. I encourage the people in my inner circle to pursue individual projects that will benefit them.

_______ 19. My inner circle is not perceived as an elite club of insiders from other leaders in the organization.

_______ 20. My inner circle exists to serve the members of it.

_______ **Total**

50 - 60 This is an area of strength. Continue growing as a leader but also spend time helping others to develop in this area.

40 - 49 This area may not be hurting you as a leader, but it isn't helping you much either. To strengthen your leadership, develop yourself in this area.

20 - 39 This is an area of weakness in your leadership. Until you grow in this area, your leadership effectiveness will be negatively impacted.

DISCUSS

Answer the following questions and discuss your answers when you meet with your mentoring group.

1. *What are the three groups of people in an organization when it comes to their responses to leadership and its impact?*

2. *Do you agree with the author's list of qualities to look for when creating an inner circle? What other qualities would you add?*

3. *In the past, how have you selected people for your inner circle?*

4. *What are the common characteristics found in the people you surround yourself with?*

5. *Have the people you've chosen to spend time with enhanced your life or made it more difficult? If they've done more harm than good, how must you change your selection process?*

6. *How do you enhance the lives of the people you spend time with? Do you challenge them and help them grow? Explain.*

7. *Up to now, how conscious have you been of surrounding yourself with strong leaders and people who will contribute to your life's journey? How will you use The Law of the Inner Circle to actively seek out additional members for your inner circle or refine your current inner circle?*

TAKE ACTION

Look at an organization in just about any profession and you can see the *Law of the Inner Circle* at work. For example, in 1997 baseball's Florida Marlins assembled an awesome group of players together as a team. What was the result? They won the World Series. But once their championship season was over, they began dismantling the team. It was a "fire sale" similar to the one that the San Diego Padres management held in the early 90s before their team was sold. The result in Florida was the same as it was in San Diego: without their key players, their inner circle, the Marlins fall in the ranks. The potential of the leader—along with the potential of the whole organization—is determined by those closest to him.

Evaluate your own inner circle. List the names of your current inner-circle members below. Next to each name, explain why that person is a part of your inner circle. What qualities and skills do they bring to the table? What areas are they more equipped in than you? How do their abilities compliment and complete your abilities? How do they support you emotionally? How do they move you closer to your goals for the team?

Inner-Circle Member	**Contributions**
____________________	______________________________
____________________	______________________________
____________________	______________________________
____________________	______________________________
____________________	______________________________
____________________	______________________________
____________________	______________________________
____________________	______________________________
____________________	______________________________
____________________	______________________________
____________________	______________________________
____________________	______________________________
____________________	______________________________
____________________	______________________________

If there are people on your list who add no value or who bring you down, you should consider moving them out of your inner circle.

After identifying your current inner-circle members and the qualities and skills they bring to the table, try to identify three more people whom you might want to add to your inner circle. Next to each person's name, list the unique skills and qualities they would bring to the group. Look for people who can fill a need that is not already being filled by another member of your inner circle. Remember that your inner circle should be made up of people from different areas of your life so you can receive a well-rounded balance of feedback and insight.

Potential Inner-Circle Member **Contributions**

12

THE LAW OF EMPOWERMENT

Only Secure Leaders Give Power to Others

The only way to make yourself indispensable is to make yourself dispensable. By becoming a secure leader who can give power away, you will make your organization more powerful. But if you disregard the *Law of Empowerment*, your potential will be limited.

READ

Just about everybody has heard of Henry Ford. He was the great innovator in the automobile industry and a legend in American business history. In 1903 he co-founded the Ford Motor Company with the belief that the future of the automobile lay in putting it within the reach of the average American. Ford said,

> I will build a motorcar for the multitude. It will be large enough for the family but small enough for the individual to run and care for. It will be constructed of the best materials, by the best men to be hired, after the simplest designs that modern engineering can devise. But it will be so low in price that no man making a good salary will be unable to own one—and enjoy with his family the blessings of hours of pleasure in God's great open spaces.

Henry Ford carried out that vision with the Model T, and it changed the face of twentieth-century American life. By 1914 Ford was producing nearly 50 percent of all automobiles in the United States. The Ford Motor Company looked like the great American success story.

However, all of Ford's story is not about positive achievement, and one of the reasons was that he didn't embrace the *Law of Empowerment*. Henry Ford was so in love with his Model T that he never wanted to change or improve it—nor did he want anyone else to do it. One day when a group of his designers surprised him by presenting him with the prototype of an improved model, Ford ripped its doors off the hinges and proceeded to destroy the car with his bare hands.

For almost twenty years the Ford Motor Company offered only the one design, the Model T, which Ford himself had developed. It wasn't until 1927 that he finally—grudgingly—agreed to offer a new car to the public. They produced the Model A, but it was incredibly far behind its competitors in technical innovations. Despite its early head start and the incredible lead it had over its competitors, the Ford Motor Company's market share kept shrinking. By 1931 it was down to only 28 percent.

Henry Ford was the antithesis of an empowering leader. He always seemed to undermine his leaders and look over the shoulders of his people. He even created a sociological department within Ford Motor Company to check up on his employees and direct their private lives. And as time went by, he became more and more eccentric.

Perhaps Ford's most peculiar dealings were with his executives, especially his son Edsel. The younger Ford had worked at the company since he was a boy. As Henry got more eccentric, Edsel worked harder to keep the company going. In fact, if it weren't for Edsel, the Ford Motor Company probably would have gone out of business in the 1930s. Henry eventually gave Edsel the presidency of the company and publicly said that Ford Motor Company's future looked bright with his leadership. Yet at the same time he undermined him and backed other leaders within the organization. And anytime a promising leader rose up in the company, Henry tore him down. As a result, the company kept losing its most promising executives. The few who stayed did so because of Edsel. They figured that someday old Henry would die, and Edsel would finally take over and set things right. But that's not what happened. In 1943 Edsel died at age forty-nine.

Edsel's oldest son, the twenty-six-year-old Henry Ford II, quickly left the Navy so that he could return to Dearborn, Michigan, and take over the company. At first he faced great opposition from his grandfather's entrenched followers. But within two years he gathered the support of several key people, received the backing of the board of directors (his mother controlled 41 percent of Ford Motor Company's stock), and convinced his grandfather to step down so that he could become president in his place.

Young Henry was taking over a company that hadn't made a profit in fifteen years. In fact, at that time, it was losing $1 million *a day!* The young president knew he was in over his head, so he began looking for leaders. Fortunately, the first group actually approached him. It was a team of ten men, headed by Col. Charles "Tex" Thornton, who had decided they wanted to work together following their service at the War Department during World War II. Their contribution to Ford Motor Company was great. In the years to come, the group produced six company vice presidents and two presidents

The second influx of leadership came with the entrance of Ernie Breech, an experienced General Motors executive and the former president of Bendix Aviation. Young Henry hired him to be Ford's executive vice-president. Although Breech held a position second to Henry's, the expectation was that he would take command and turn the company around. And he did. Breech quickly brought in over 150 outstanding executives from General Motors, and by 1949, Ford Motor Company was back on a roll again. In that year the company sold over a million Fords, Mercuries, and Lincolns—the best sales since the Model A.

If Henry Ford II had lived by the *Law of Empowerment,* the Ford Motor Company might have grown enough to eventually overtake General Motors and become the number-one car company again. But only secure leaders are able to give power to others. Henry felt threatened. The success of Tex Thornton, Ernie Breech, and Lewis Crusoe, a legendary GM executive Breech had brought into the company, made Henry worry about his own place at Ford. His position was based not on influence but on his name and his family's control of company stock.

So Henry began pitting one top executive against another. He would invite Thornton to his office and encourage him to criticize fellow executive Crusoe. After a while Crusoe got fed up with Thornton's insubordination and demanded that Breech fire him, which he did. Then Ford started backing Crusoe, who worked for Breech.

This became a pattern in the leadership of Henry Ford II. Anytime an executive gained power and influence, Henry would undercut the person's authority by either moving him to a position with less clout, supporting the executive's subordinates, or publically humiliating him. This continued all the days Henry II was at Ford. As one Ford president, Lee Iacocca, said after leaving the company, "Henry Ford, as I would learn firsthand, had a nasty habit of getting rid of strong leaders."

Iacocca said that Henry Ford II once described his leadership philosophy to him, years before Iacocca himself became a target of it. Ford said, "If a guy works for you, don't let him get too comfortable. Don't let him get cozy or set in his ways. Always do the opposite of what he expects. Keep your people anxious and off-balance."[1]

Both Henry Fords failed to abide by the *Law of Empowerment*. Rather than finding leaders, building them up, giving them resources, authority, and responsibility, and then turning them loose to achieve, they alternately encouraged and undermined their best people because of their own insecurity. And as a result, the company suffered.

OBSERVE

Theodore Roosevelt said, "The best executive is the one who has sense enough to pick good men to do what he wants done, and the self-restraint enough to keep from meddling with them while they do it."

1. *Why did the Ford Company lose its market share?*

2. *How did both Henry Ford and Henry Ford II violate the Law of Empowerment? How did this affect their company?*

3. *Give an example of how a leader in your profession or area of service has violated the Law of Empowerment, and how it has effected his or her organization.*

4. *Give an example of how a leader in your profession or area of service has exemplified the Law of Empowerment, and how it has affected his or her organization.*

LEARN

Only empowered people can reach their potential. When a leader can't or won't empower others, then he creates barriers within the organization that people simply cannot overcome. If the barriers remain long enough, then the people either give up, or they move to another organization where they can maximize their potential.

Why do some leaders violate the *Law of Empowerment*? Take a look at several common reasons:

Desire for Job Security

The greatest enemy of empowerment is the desire for job security. A weak leader worries that if he helps subordinates, he will become dispensable. But the truth is that the only way to make yourself indispensable is to make yourself dispensable. In other words, if you are able to continually empower others and help them develop so that they become capable of taking over your job, you will become so valuable to the organization that you become indispensable. That's one of the great paradoxes of the *Law of Empowerment*.

Resistance to Change

Nobel Prize-winning author John Steinbeck said, "It is the nature of man as he grows older to protest against change, particularly change for the better." By its very nature, empowerment brings constant change, because it encourages people to grow and innovate. Change is the price of progress.

Lack of Self-Worth

Many people gain their personal value and esteem from their work or positions. Threaten to change either of them, and you threaten their self-worth. On the other hand, author Buck Rogers says, "To those who have confidence in themselves, change is a stimulus because they believe one person can make a difference and influence what goes on around them. These people are the doers and motivators." They are also the empowerers.

Only secure leaders are able to give themselves away. Mark Twain once said that great things can happen when you don't care who gets the credit. But you can take that a step further. I believe the greatest things happen *only* when you give others the credit. That's the *Law of Empowerment* in action.

EVALUATE

Rate your own leadership by placing the number 1, 2, or 3 next to each of the following statements: 1 = Never 2 = Sometimes 3 = Always

_______ 1. It's easy for me to share my authority and power.

_______ 2. When I share authority with someone, I also try to help develop his or her leadership ability.

_______ 3. I allow the people I share authority with to make a few mistakes.

_______ 4. I trust and believe in my key leaders.

_______ 5. I encourage risk taking within the context of our leadership culture.

_______ 6. I will tolerate a few mistakes within our leadership culture.

_______ 7. I cultivate and encourage an innovative spirit.

_______ 8. I provide continued high-quality training for the leaders of the organization.

_______ 9. I know that the basis of my leadership is not based on my authority, and my actions reflect this belief.

_______ 10. The key players around me would assess me as being a secure and confident leader.

_______ 11. My key leaders express gratitude for the opportunities I've made available to them.

_______ 12. I am willing to give up areas of responsibility to my team.

_______ 13. I help to develop the leaders around me.

_______ 14. My subordinates see me as their biggest cheerleader when they have great ideas and personal successes.

_______ 15. Team members express that they feel I believe in them more than they believe in themselves.

_______ 16. I encourage my team members to develop a personal growth plan, and I am willing to act as their coach.

_______ 17. I will approve funds so my team members can be better trained.

_______ 18. People seem to want to be on my team.

_______ 19. I give more credit than I seek. I would rather see my team applauded than me personally.

_______ 20. I intentionally seek ways for my key players to receive opportunities for growth and advancement.

_______ **Total**

50 - 60 This is an area of strength. Continue growing as a leader but also spend time helping others to develop in this area.

40 - 49 This area may not be hurting you as a leader, but it isn't helping you much either. To strengthen your leadership, develop yourself in this area.

20 - 39 This is an area of weakness in your leadership. Until you grow in this area, your leadership effectiveness will be negatively impacted.

DISCUSS

Answer the following questions and discuss your answers when you meet with your mentoring group.

1. *Why do some leaders violate the Law of Empowerment?*

2. *Which of the three reasons why leaders don't share their authority is most prevalent in your profession or area of service? Give examples.*

3. *How has a leader's resistance to the Law of Empowerment affected you and your teams in the past?*

4. *In the past, how has a leader empowered you? What was the result?*

5. *Do you agree that the only way to become indispensable is to become dispensable? Explain.*

6. *Are you more likely to resist empowering others due to your desire for job security, resistance to change, lack of self-worth, or another reason? How can you get past this leadership obstacle?*

7. *What are some ways you will empower others in your current position?*

TAKE ACTION

One-time vice-presidential candidate Admiral James B. Stockdale said,

> Leadership must be based on goodwill. . . . It means obvious and wholehearted commitment to helping followers. . . . What we need for leaders are men of heart who are so helpful that they, in effect, do away with the need of their jobs. But leaders like that are never out of a job, never out of followers. Strange as it sounds, great leaders gain authority by giving it away.

This week, find one situation in which you can share you authority with someone else. It could be letting your child plan a family event for the weekend or giving someone on your team authority over a project. Answer the following questions throughout the week in order to evaluate the experience.

I shared my authority with ____________________________________,
by empowering him or her to ____________________________________ .

1. *Why did you choose this person to share your authority with?*

____

____

____

____

2. *What were your initial concerns when sharing your authority with someone else?*

____

____

____

____

____

____

3. *How did this person react to your offer?*

4. *What were some of the challenges this person faced with the project, task, or decision?*

5. *How did you encourage this person?*

6. *How did you help that individual grow as a leader?*

7. *What was the outcome of the project, task, or decision?*

8. *How was sharing authority beneficial to you and to the other person?*

13

THE LAW OF REPRODUCTION

It Takes a Leader to Raise Up a Leader

A few years ago at my leadership conference I took the time to do some informal polling of the audience. My goal was to find out what prompted the men and women who attend to become leaders. The results of the survey were as follows:

How They Became Leaders	
Natural Gifting	10%
Result of Crisis	5%
Influence of Another Leader	85%

If you've ever given much thought to the origins of leadership, then you're probably not surprised by those figures. It's true that a few people step into leadership because their organizations experience a crisis, and they are compelled to do something about it. Another small group is comprised of people with such great natural gifting and instincts that they are able to navigate their way into leadership on their own. But more than four out of five leaders that you meet will have emerged as leaders because of the impact made on them by established leaders who mentored them. That happens because of the *Law of Reproduction*: It takes a leader to raise up a leader.

READ

When I originally wrote *The 21 Irrefutable Laws of Leadership* in 1998, I did some research. At that time the development and mentoring of nearly half of the head coaches in the NFL could be traced back to two outstanding former pro football leaders: Bill Walsh and Tom Landry. Nine NFL head coaches spent a year or longer working for three-time Super Bowl champion Bill Walsh or for one of the top assistants he trained. And five NFL coaches have a direct or indirect mentoring connection with two-time Super Bowl winner Tom Landry or one of the men he trained (see chart).

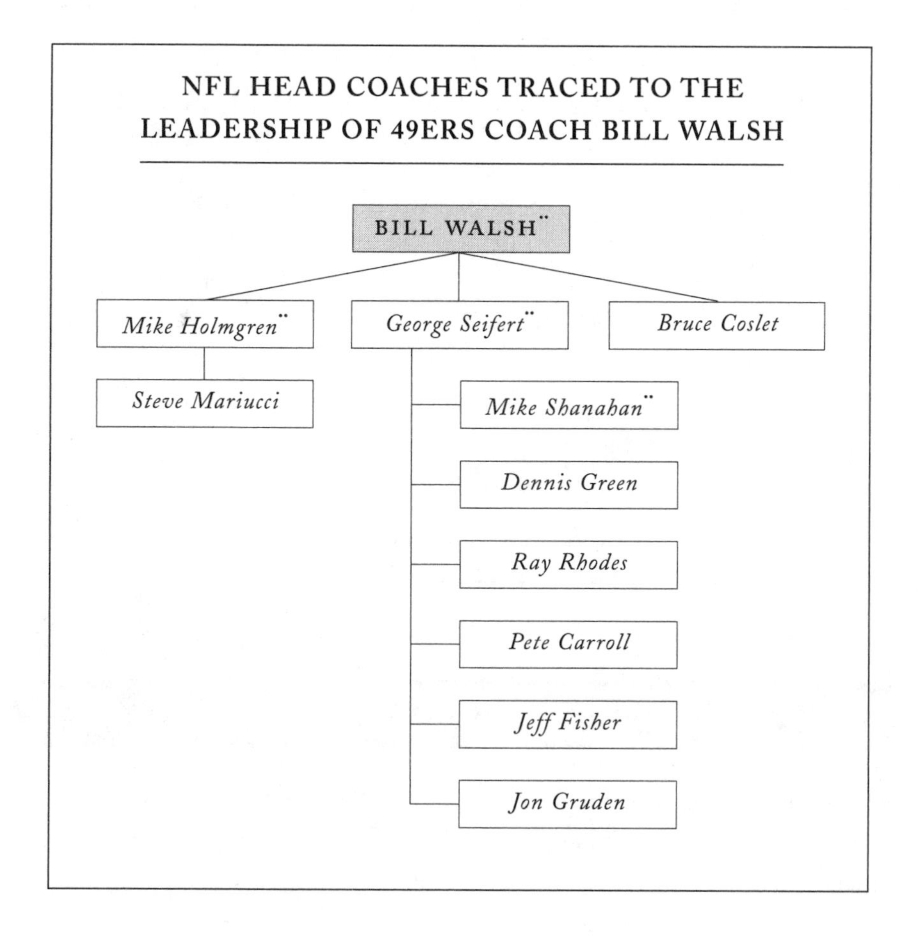

Just about every successful coach in the NFL has spent time working with another strong leader who helped to teach and model for him. In addition to the ones with a Walsh or Landry connection, there are other NFL examples: Dave Wannstedt worked for two-time Super Bowl champion Jimmy Johnson, and head coaches Bill Cowher and Tony Dungy spent significant time working with Marty Schottenheimer of the Kansas City Chiefs.

Could an unsuccessful coach produce such results? No. It takes a person who has done it himself. And just as it takes a winning coach to produce other winning coaches, it takes a leader to raise up other leaders.

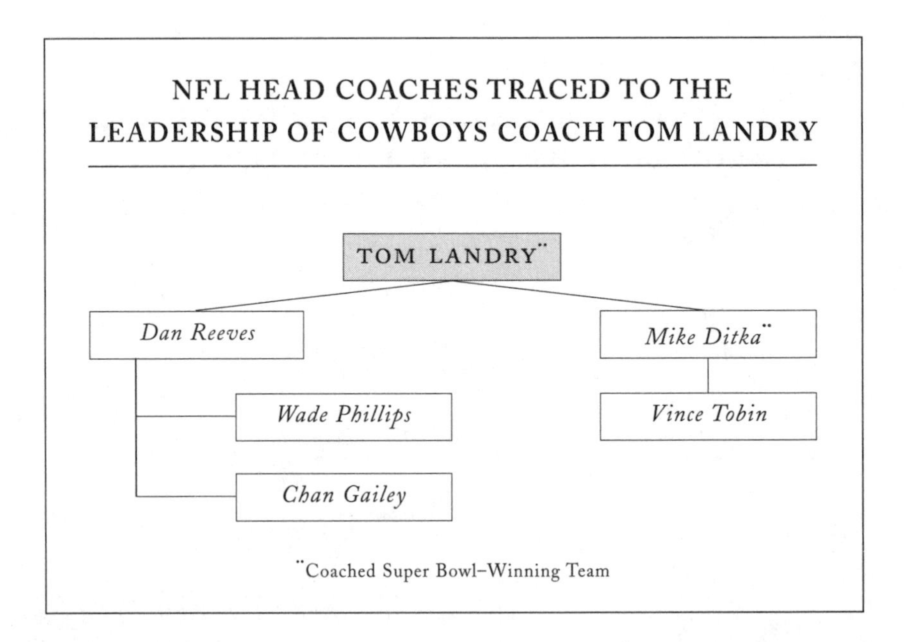

OBSERVE

Only leaders are capable of developing other leaders. People cannot give to others what they themselves do not possess. Followers simply cannot develop leaders.

1. *What prompted you to enter leadership?*

2. *What do most successful coaches in the NFL have in common?*

3. *How do the leaders in your profession or area of service support the Law Reproduction or disprove it?*

4. *Who in your profession or area of service is actively raising up other leaders? How are they doing this?*

LEARN

Just because a person is a leader, it does not necessarily mean that he or she will raise up other leaders. For every Bill Walsh, George Seifert, or Tom Landry, there is a Vince Lombardi—a person who is a great coach and leader in his own right, but who doesn't raise up other great coaches to follow in his footsteps.

Why don't all leaders develop others? There are many reasons. Sometimes they just don't recognize the tremendous *value* of developing leaders. Others may focus so much attention on their followers and give them so much that they don't have anything left for their key staff. I suspect that was the case with Vince Lombardi. For other leaders the real problem may be insecurity. Only secure leaders give power to others.

The only way you will be able to develop other leaders is if you become a leader yourself. If you've already taken those first steps, that's great. You're in a position to begin raising up other leaders. As you get started, keep in mind that leaders who develop leaders . . .

1. See the Big Picture

Every effective leadership mentor makes the development of leaders one of his highest priorities in life. He knows that the potential of the organization depends on the growth of its leadership. The more leaders there are, the greater its chance of success.

2. Attract Potential Leaders

You've probably heard the old Ross Perot quote: "Leaders don't flock. You have to find them one at a time." That's true. But if you first develop your own leadership qualities, you will be capable of attracting people with leadership potential. When you do that and also earn their respect, you will get the opportunity to develop them into better leaders.

3. Create an Eagle Environment

An environment where leadership is valued and taught becomes a great asset to a leadership mentor. It not only attracts "eagles," but it helps them learn to fly. An eagle environment is one where the leader casts vision, offers incentives, encourages creativity, allows risks, and provides accountability. Do that long enough with enough people, and you'll develop a leadership culture where eagles do begin to flock.

Once you understand the *Law of Reproduction*, you recognize the incredible impact it has on an organization. If a company has poor leaders, what little leadership it has will only get worse. If a company has great leaders—and they are reproducing themselves—then the leadership just keeps getting better and better.

EVALUATE

Rate your own leadership by placing the number 1, 2, or 3 next to each of the following statements: 1 = Never 2 = Sometimes 3 = Always

_______ 1. I am a developer of people.

_______ 2. I find great joy in seeing others around me rise above my own capabilities.

_______ 3. I mentor at least two individuals.

_______ 4. The people I am mentoring show signs of growth both personally and professionally.

_______ 5. Mentoring and investing in other people's lives is important to me.

_______ 6. I see people for who they are more than what they can do for me.

_______ 7. I am willing to invest significant amounts of time and energy into the key people around me.

_______ 8. My visions and dreams are too big to accomplish by myself.

_______ 9. I think long-term process more than short-term project when it comes to people development.

_______ 10. My motive for investing in others is more about the mission or cause than my own personal legacy.

_______ 11. I realize the tight correlation between my competence and my character when it comes to reproducing my leadership.

_______ 12. I have realistic expectations for the people I'm developing.

_______ 13. I am patient with the people I'm investing in.

_______ 14. I am available to the people I'm mentoring.

_______ 15. I am specific and intentional about the points of change and growth I want to see happen in those I'm mentoring.

_______ 16. I spend more time on developing the strengths of those whom I mentor than focusing on improving their weaknesses.

_______ 17. I am committed to a lifetime of personal growth.

_______ 18. I make significant contributions to the lives of others.

_______ 19. My motivation in mentoring is to make others better, not make me look better.

_______ 20. I am on the lookout for people with whom I share a natural connection, who are responsive to my leadership, and who I can invest in.

_______ **Total**

50 - 60 This is an area of strength. Continue growing as a leader but also spend time helping others to develop in this area.

40 - 49 This area may not be hurting you as a leader, but it isn't helping you much either. To strengthen your leadership, develop yourself in this area.

20 - 39 This is an area of weakness in your leadership. Until you grow in this area, your leadership effectiveness will be negatively impacted.

DISCUSS

Answer the following questions and discuss your answers when you meet with your mentoring group.

1. *What must you do before you can develop other leaders?*

2. *What are three things that leaders who develop leaders do?*

3. *Do you agree with the author that we reproduce what we are? Explain.*

4. *How have you benefited from the advice or instructions of other leaders?*

5. *Is mentoring a part of your life? Why or why not?*

6. *What are you doing to become a better leader?*

7. *How close or far away from mentoring someone else are you? Why?*

8. *What will you do now to develop other leaders?*

TAKE ACTION

I was very fortunate growing up because I lived in the household of a great leader: my father, Melvin Maxwell. Every day of my early life, I learned lessons about working with people, understanding priorities, developing myself through a personal growth plan, and paying the price of leadership. Some of what I learned came from his teaching. But even more of it came from being around him, watching him interact with others, and learning how he thought. As a result, by the time I went to college, I already had pretty good intuition and understood leadership better than most of my peers. Since then, I've spent my life continuing to learn about leadership. And I've sought out great leaders to mentor me so that I could keep learning.

If you want to continue developing as a leader, you should do the same. Spend time with the best leaders you can find. If you're just starting out, you may want to spend time with people in your own field so that you can master the basics of your profession. But once you have that foundation, learn leadership from people in many different professions. I've learned from businesspeople, pastors, politicians, generals, ballplayers, entrepreneurs—you name it. No matter what the profession, the principles of leadership remain the same.

List below the name of the person you will ask to become your mentor. Also list the name of one person you will commit to mentoring. After each person's name, fill in the related phrases. Then set up a time to meet with each person in the next few weeks.

My Mentor: ______________________________

Why I chose this person: ______________________________

____

How I expect to change: ______________________________

____

____

____

Areas I want him or her to mentor me in:
1. ______________________________
2. ______________________________
3. ______________________________

I will meet with this person ______________________
We will meet ________ (once each, every other) week for ______months.

I Will Mentor:______________________________
Why I chose this person:

____

____

How I will equip and invest in this person:

____

____

Areas where I want to help him or her grow:
1. ______________________________
2. ______________________________
3. ______________________________

I will begin meeting with this person on ________________
We will meet ________ (once each, every other) week for ______ months.

14

THE LAW OF BUY-IN

People Buy Into the Leader, Then the Vision

Most people have it backwards. They believe that if the cause is good enough, people will automatically buy into it and follow. But that's not how leadership really works. People don't at first follow worthy causes. They follow worthy leaders who promote worthwhile causes. People will buy into you before they buy into your vision. Having an understanding of the *Law of Buy-In* changes your whole approach to leading people.

READ

In the fall of 1997, a few members of my staff and I had the opportunity to travel to India and teach four leadership conferences. India is an amazing country, full of contradictions. It's a place of beauty with warm and generous people, yet at the same time millions and millions of its inhabitants live in the worst poverty imaginable. It was there that I was reminded of the *Law of Buy-In*.

I'll never forget when our plane landed in Delhi. As we exited the airport it was like we had been transported to another planet. There were crowds everywhere. People on bicycles, in cars, on camels and elephants. People on the streets, some sleeping right on the sidewalks. Animals roamed free no matter where we were. And everything was in motion. As we drove along the main street toward our hotel, I also noticed something else. Banners. No matter where we looked, we could see banners celebrating India's fifty years of liberty, along with huge pictures of one man: Mahatma Gandhi.

Today, people take for granted that Gandhi was a great leader. But the story of his leadership is a marvelous study in the *Law of Buy-In*. Mohandas K. Gandhi, called Mahatma (which means "great soul"), was educated in London. After finishing his education in law, he traveled back to India, and then to South Africa. There he worked for twenty years as a barrister and political activist. And in that time he developed as a leader, fighting for the rights of Indians and other minorities who were oppressed and discriminated against by South Africa's apartheid government.

By the time he returned to India in 1914, Gandhi was very well-known and highly respected among his countrymen. Over the next several years, as he led protests and strikes around the country, people rallied to him and looked to him more and more for leadership. In 1920—a mere six years after returning to India—he was elected president of the All India Home Rule League.

The most remarkable thing about Gandhi isn't that he became their leader, but that he was able to change the people's vision for obtaining freedom. Before he began leading them, the people used violence in an effort to achieve their goals. For years riots against the British establishment had been common. But Gandhi's vision for change in India was based on nonviolent civil disobedience. He once said, "Nonviolence is the greatest force at the disposal of mankind. It is mightier than the mightiest weapon of destruction devised by the ingenuity of man."

Gandhi challenged the people to meet oppression with peaceful disobedience and noncooperation. Even when the British military massacred over a thousand people at Amritsar in 1919, Gandhi called the people to stand but without fighting back. Rallying everyone to his way of thinking wasn't easy. But because the people had come to buy into him as their leader, they embraced his vision. And then they followed him faithfully. He asked them not to fight, and eventually they stopped fighting. When he called for everyone to burn their foreign-made clothes and start wearing nothing but home-spun material, millions of people started doing it. When he decided that a March to the Sea to protest the Salt Act would be their rallying point for civil disobedience against the British, the nation's leaders followed him the two-hundred miles to the city of Dandi, where they were arrested by government representatives.

Their struggle for independence was slow and painful, but Gandhi's leadership was strong enough to deliver on the promise of his vision. In 1947 India gained home rule. Because the people had bought into Gandhi, they accepted his vision. And once they had embraced the vision, they were able to carry it out. That's how the *Law of Buy-In* works. The leader finds the dream, and then the people. The people find the leader and then the dream.

OBSERVE

Every message that people receive is filtered through the messenger who delivers it. If you consider the messenger to be credible, then you believe the message has value. That's one of the reasons actors and athletes are hired as promoters of products. Once people have bought into someone, they are willing to give his vision a chance.

1. *Why did people buy into Gandhi's vision for nonviolent protest? How had he established himself as a leader?*

2. *How do you think the people would have reacted to Gandhi's suggestion of nonviolent protest if he had not already established himself as a leader?*

3. *Whose vision have you bought into? Why?*

4. *Who in your profession or area of service seems to have the ability to rally people around their vision? What have they done to deserve such a response?*

LEARN

You cannot separate the leader from the cause he or she promotes. It cannot be done, no matter how hard you try. It's not an either/or proposition. The two always go together. Take a look at the following table. It shows how people react to a leader and his vision under different circumstances:

Leader	+	Vision	=	Result
Don't Buy In		Don't Buy In		Get Another Leader
Don't Buy In		Buy In		Get Another Leader
Buy In		Don't Buy In		Get Another Vision
Buy In		Buy In		Get Behind the Leader

When Followers Don't Like the Leader or the Vision, They Look for Another Leader

It's easy to understand the reaction of people when they don't like the leader or the vision. They simply don't follow. But they also do something else: they start looking for another leader. It's a no-win situation.

When Followers Don't Like the Leader but They Do Like the Vision, They Still Look for Another Leader

You may be surprised by this. Even though people may think a cause is good, if they don't like the leader, they will go out and find another one. That's one of the reasons coaches change teams so often in professional sports. The vision for any team always stays the same: Everyone wants to win a championship. But the players don't always believe in their leader. And when they don't, what happens? The owners don't fire all of the players. They fire the leader and bring in someone they hope the players will buy into.

When Followers Like the Leader but Not the Vision, They Change the Vision

Even when people don't like a leader's vision, if they've already bought into him, they will keep following him. You see this often in politics. For example, in the past, the National Organization of Women (NOW) has spoken out strongly against sexual harassment. But when President Clinton was accused of it by Paula Jones, NOW continued to support him. Why? It's not because they suddenly think sexual harassment is acceptable. They have chosen to put their own agenda on hold in order to keep supporting the leader they've already bought into.

When a group of followers doesn't agree with their leader's vision, they react in many different ways: Sometimes they work to convince their leader to change his vision. Sometimes they abandon their own point of view and adopt his. Other times they find some sort of compromise. But as long as they still buy into the leader, they won't out-and-out reject him. They will keep following.

When Followers Like the Leader and the Vision, They Get Behind Both

When the leader and the vision line up, people will get behind both. And they will follow their leader no matter how bad conditions get or how much the odds are stacked against them. That's why the Indian people in Gandhi's day refused to fight back as soldiers mowed them down. It's what inspired the U.S. space program to fulfill John F. Kennedy's vision and put a man on the moon. It's the reason people continued to have hope and keep alive the dream of Martin Luther King Jr., even after he was gunned down. It is what continues to inspire followers to keep running the race, even when they feel they've hit the wall and given everything they've got.

As a leader, if you have a great vision and a worthy cause, that alone is not enough to get people to follow you. First you have to become a better leader. You must get your people to buy into *you* first. That is the price you've got to pay if you want your vision to have a chance of becoming a reality.

EVALUATE

Rate your own leadership by placing the number 1, 2, or 3 next to each of the following statements: 1 = Never 2 = Sometimes 3 = Always

_______ 1. People follow my leadership easily and rarely with hesitation.

_______ 2. I know exactly where I'm headed and how the people on my team need to participate to accomplish the task or mission.

_______ 3. My vision is crystal clear, and I have a written plan to make it happen.

_______ 4. People tend to accept my opinions.

_______ 5. Key leaders connect with me.

_______ 6. The people closest to me trust me fully and without reservation.

_______ 7. The key leaders around me not only support me, they take initiative to show their support.

_______ 8. I live a personal lifestyle worthy of the people's trust and respect.

_______ 9. I am open, honest, and transparent with the people I work with.

_______ 10. The people in my organization see the value I bring as a leader.

_______ 11. I treat people with dignity and respect.

_______ 12. I am able to connect with most people.

_______ 13. The people on my team know that I have their best interests at heart.

_______ 14. I am generous with my time with the people I work with.

_______ 15. I put other people's needs before my own.

_______ 16. My actions build trust.

_______ 17. I am clear on my vision and how to achieve it.

_______ 18. The people on my team and other key leaders support me even in challenging times.

_______ 19. I pay close attention to what the people on my team care about and focus on meeting their needs.

_______ 20. The people in my organization respect me and show interest in my opinions and desires.

_______ **Total**

50 - 60 This is an area of strength. Continue growing as a leader but also spend time helping others to develop in this area.

40 - 49 This area may not be hurting you as a leader, but it isn't helping you much either. To strengthen your leadership, develop yourself in this area.

20 - 39 This is an area of weakness in your leadership. Until you grow in this area, your leadership effectiveness will be negatively impacted.

DISCUSS

Answer the following questions and discuss your answers when you meet with your mentoring group.

1. *How do leaders and followers differ when it comes to supporting a vision?*

2. *Under what circumstances would a follower look for another leader?*

3. *Why might you stay with a leader whose vision began to depart from what it was when you began following him or her?*

4. *Do you agree with the author that, "The leader finds the dream and then the people. The people find the leader and then the dream"? Explain.*

5. *Have you ever cast vision and not had people buy into it and follow? How might your leadership have affected the response you received? Explain.*

6. *Up to now, did you approach leadership with the understanding that people must first buy into you before they will buy into your vision? Give an example of your previous leadership approach to casting vision and rallying followers.*

7. *What will you do to increase the potential Buy-In for your vision?*

TAKE ACTION

As a leader, you don't earn any points for failing in a noble cause. You don't get credit for being "right." Your success is measured by your ability to actually take the people where they need to go. But you can do that only if the people first buy into you as a leader.

Think about some problem, project or goal that you have a vision for. Then think about who could help you to realize that vision. During the coming weeks, intentionally build relationships with those people, and do what you can to help them be successful. Only after you have invested in them should you share your vision. Once you have, note how they respond.

Vision: ____
Person who can help me realize my vision: ____________________
I will intentionally build a relationship with this person by _________

Ways I can add value to them:
1. ____
2. ____
3. ____

The level of my connection before I shared my vision was _________

How this person responded to my vision: ______________________

15

THE LAW OF VICTORY

Leaders Find a Way for the Team to Win

Have you ever thought about what separates the leaders who achieve victory from those who suffer defeat? What does it take to be a winner? It's hard to put a finger on the quality that separates a winner from a loser. Every leadership situation is different. Every crisis has its own challenges. But one thing victorious leaders share is an inability to accept defeat. The alternative to winning seems totally unacceptable to them, so they figure out what must be done to achieve victory, and then they go after it with everything at their disposal.

READ

Crisis seems to bring out the best—and the worst—in leaders. During World War II, two great leaders who practiced the *Law of Victory* emerged for the Allies: British Prime Minister Winston Churchill and U.S. President Franklin Roosevelt. They prevented Adolf Hitler from crushing Europe and remaking it according to his own vision.

On his side of the Atlantic Ocean, Winston Churchill inspired the British people to resist Hitler. Long before he became Prime Minister in 1940, Churchill spoke out against the Nazis. He seemed like the lone critic in 1932 when he said,

"Do not delude yourselves. . . . Do not believe that all Germany is asking for is equal status. . . . They are looking for weapons and when they have them, believe me, they will ask for the return of lost territories or colonies."

Churchill continued to speak out against the Nazis. And when Hitler annexed Austria in 1938, Churchill said to members of the House of Commons:

> For five years I have talked to the House on these matters—not with very great success. I have watched this famous island descending incontinently, fecklessly, the stairway which leads to a dark gulf. . . Now is the time at last to rouse the nation. Perhaps it is the last time it can be roused with a chance of preventing war, or with a chance of coming through with victory should our effort to prevent war fail.

Unfortunately, Prime Minister Neville Chamberlain and the other leaders of Britain did not rise up and make a stand against Hitler. And more of Europe fell to the Nazis.

By mid 1940 most of Europe was under Germany's thumb. But then something happened that may have changed the history of the free world. The leadership of England fell to Winston Churchill. He refused to buckle under Nazi threats. For over a year Britain stood alone facing the threat of German invasion. When Hitler indicated that he wanted to make a deal with England, Churchill defied him. When Germany began bombing England, the British stood strong. And all the while, Churchill looked for a way to gain victory.

Time after time, he rallied the British people. It began with his first speech after becoming Prime Minister. He said:

> We have before us an ordeal of the most grievous kind. We have before us many, many long months of struggle and of suffering. You ask what is our policy? I will say: It is to wage war, by sea, land and air, with all our might and with all the strength that God can give us; to wage war against a monstrous tyranny, never surpassed in the dark, lamentable catalogue of human crime. That is our policy. You ask, What is our aim? I answer in one word: Victory—victory at all costs, victory in spite of all terror, victory, however long and hard the road may be; for without victory, there is no survival.[1]

Meanwhile, Churchill did everything in his power to prevail. He deployed troops in the Mediterranean against Mussolini's forces. Although he hated communism, he allied himself with Stalin and the Soviets, sending them aid even when Britain's own supplies were threatened and its survival hung in the balance. And he developed a personal relationship with Franklin Roosevelt. Though the President of the United States was reluctant to enter the war, Churchill worked to build his relationship with him, hoping to change it from one of friendship and mutual respect to a full-fledged war alliance. And in time it paid off. On the day the Japanese bombed Pearl Harbor, ushering America into the war, Churchill said to himself, "So we have won after all."

Prior to December of 1941, Franklin Roosevelt had already been practicing the *Law of Victory* for decades. In fact it is a hallmark of his entire life. He had found a way to achieve political victory while winning over crippling polio. When he was elected President and became responsible for pulling the American people out of the Great Depression, it was just another impossible situation that he learned how to fight through. And fight he did. Through the 1930s, the country was slowly recovering.

By the time the Nazis were battling in Europe, the stakes were high. Pulitzer Prize–winning historian Arthur Schlesinger Jr. said, "The Second World War found democracy fighting for its life. By 1941 there were only a dozen or so democratic states left on earth. But great leadership emerged in time to rally the democratic cause." The team of Roosevelt and Churchill provided that leadership like a one-two punch. Just as the Prime Minister had rallied England, the President brought together the American people and united them in a common cause as no one ever had before nor has since.

To those two leaders, victory was the only option. If they had accepted anything less, the world would be a very different place today. Schlesinger says,

> Take a look at our present world. It is manifestly not Adolf Hitler's world. His Thousand-Year Reich turned out to have a brief and bloody run of a dozen years. It is manifestly not Joseph Stalin's world. That ghastly world self-destructed before our eyes. Nor is it Winston Churchill's world. . . The world we live in is Franklin Roosevelt's world.[2]

Without Churchill and England, all of Europe would have fallen. Without Roosevelt and the United States, it might never have been reclaimed for freedom. But not even an Adolf Hitler and army of the Third Reich could stand against two leaders dedicated to the *Law of Victory*.

OBSERVE

When the pressure is on, great leaders are at their best. Whatever is inside them comes to the surface and works for or against them.

1. *How do the words of Winston Churchill reflect the Law of Victory?*

2. *How do the actions of Winston Churchill reflect the Law of Victory?*

3. *How do you think Franklin Roosevelt's prior commitment to the Law of Victory factored into how he led America during WWII?*

4. *Identify and describe someone in your profession or area of service who reflects the Law of Victory.*

LEARN

Whether you're looking at a sports team, an army, a business, or a non-profit organization, victory is possible as long as you have three components:

1. Unity of Vision

Teams succeed only when the players have a unified vision, no matter how much talent or potential there is. A team doesn't win the championship if its players have different agendas. That's true in professional sports. It's true in business. It's true in churches.

I learned this lesson back in high school when I was a junior on the varsity basketball team. We had a very talented group of kids, and we had been picked to win the state championship. But we had a problem. The juniors and seniors on the team refused to work together. It got so bad that the coach eventually gave up trying to get us to play together and divided us into two different squads for our games. In the end the team did horribly. Why? We didn't share a common vision.

2. Diversity of Skills

It almost goes without saying that the team needs diversity of skills. Can you imagine a whole hockey team of goalies? Or a football team of quarterbacks? It doesn't make sense. In the same way, organizations require diverse talents to succeed, each player taking his or her part.

3. A Leader Dedicated to Victory and Raising Players to their Potential

It's true that having good players with diverse skills is important. As former Notre Dame head football coach Lou Holtz says, "You've got to have great athletes to win, I don't care who the coach is. You can't win without good athletes, but you can lose with them. This is where coaching makes the difference." In other words, you also require leadership to achieve victory. Unity of vision doesn't happen spontaneously. The right players with the proper diversity of talent don't come together on their own. It takes a leader to make those things happen, and it takes a leader to provide the motivation, empowerment, and direction required to win.

EVALUATE

Rate your own leadership by placing the number 1, 2, or 3 next to each of the following statements: 1 = Never 2 = Sometimes 3 = Always

_______ 1. I experience success as a leader.

_______ 2. I overcome and learn from my defeats, setbacks or failures.

_______ 3. I work in environments where I am best suited to lead the team to victory.

_______ 4. I function well under pressure.

_______ 5. After a setback I recover quickly.

_______ 6. Change is not only accepted but quickly embraced by the key leaders in our organization.

_______ 7. I will implement something even if all the "bugs and kinks" aren't worked out yet.

_______ 8. I not only cast vision, I give the strategy for implementing that vision.

_______ 9. My leadership attitude is: There is no Plan B. We will accomplish our primary mission.

_______ 10. I am willing to make significant personal sacrifices in order to achieve the overall mission.

_______ 11. All the leaders on my team possess a committed and "fighting" spirit to see victory achieved.

_______ 12. The majority of my team is willing to give up their rights and even "sacrifice" a small win for themselves in order to attain the big-picture victory.

_______ 13. I can carve a path through defeat in order to achieve ultimate victory.

_______ 14. There is a direct correlation between my personal preparation and readiness as a leader and the success of my team.

_______ 15. We celebrate victories by including as many people in the organization as possible and use the victory to launch us toward the next big goal.

_______ 16. I focus on the priorities that lead to success rather than giving in to the "tyranny of the urgent."

_______ 17. We celebrate both small and large victories.

_______ 18. I view mistakes and failures as stepping stones to success.

_______ 19. I insist that we all focus more on getting the job done than who gets the credit.

_______ 20. I expect high-caliber and competent leadership from myself and those around me.

_______ **Total**

50 - 60 This is an area of strength. Continue growing as a leader but also spend time helping others to develop in this area.

40 - 49 This area may not be hurting you as a leader, but it isn't helping you much either. To strengthen your leadership, develop yourself in this area.

20 - 39 This is an area of weakness in your leadership. Until you grow in this area, your leadership effectiveness will be negatively impacted.

DISCUSS

Answer the following questions and discuss your answers when you meet with your mentoring group.

1. *What are the three components that the author believes are necessary for victory.*

2. *Are there other factors the author didn't mention? If so, name them.*

3. *Has anyone in your organization consistently demonstrated the Law of Victory?*

4. *Which of the three components of victory do you think your team strongly displays? Explain.*

5. *How can your team strengthen its Unity of Vision?*

6. *As a leader, how can you express your dedication to victory?*

7. *How can you help those on your team reach their potential?*

TAKE ACTION

You and each person on your team have a unique set of gifts, talents, and training. This week, if your team has not already, take a personality test such as DISC or Myers Briggs. Then have each person, including yourself, fill out the survey below. Individually review each person's test and survey answers and discuss with him or her the part he or she plays on the team. Also, let the team know about opportunities that are available to them to improve or learn specific skills.

1. What job task do you enjoy doing the most? Why?

___
___
___

2. What job task do you least enjoy? Why?

___
___
___

3. What are your hobbies and interests?

___
___
___

4. What is your formal training? (degrees, certifications, classes taken)

___
___
___

5. Outside of your obvious job skills, what other skills or training do you have?

___
___
___

6. In what area do you think you would best serve the team?

7. What are your career goals?

8. How do you benefit from being a member of this team?

9. How does the team benefit from having you as a member?

10. What would it take for you to become a player on the team who consistently personifies The Law of Victory?

16

THE LAW OF THE BIG MO

Momentum Is a Leader's Best Friend

One of the greatest challenges any leader faces is creating change in an organization. The key is momentum—what I call the Big Mo. Just as every sailor knows that you can't steer a ship that isn't moving forward, strong leaders understand that to change direction, you first have to create forward progress—and that takes the *Law of the Big Mo.*

READ

I saw a movie several years ago called *Stand and Deliver.* Maybe you've seen it too. It's about a real-life teacher named Jaime Escalante who worked at Garfield High School in East Los Angeles, California. The movie focused on Escalante's ability to teach, but the real story is actually a great study in the *Law of the Big Mo.*

At age forty-three, Escalante was hired by Garfield High School to teach computer science. But when he arrived at Garfield on the first day of class, he found that there was no funding for computers. And because his degree was in mathematics, he would instead be teaching basic math. Disappointed, he went in search of his first class, hoping that his dream of making a difference wasn't slipping through his fingers.

The change from computers to math turned out to be the least of Escalante's problems. The school, which had been quiet during his summertime interview, was now in chaos. Discipline was nonexistent. Fights seemed to break out continually. Trash and graffiti were everywhere. Students—and even outsiders from the neighborhood—roamed all over the campus throughout the day. Escalante even discovered that Mr. Avilez, the school's liberal principal, was actually *encouraging* gang recognition on campus. Escalante knew that the students were doomed if the school didn't change. They were all sliding backwards fast, and they needed something to move them forward.

The break came as a result of what looked like a major setback: When the school was informed that it was in danger of losing its accreditation, the district removed principal Alex Avilez and replaced him with a better leader, Paul Possemato. He immediately cleaned up the school, discouraged gang activity, and chased outsiders from the campus. Though he was at the school only two years, the principal saved Garfield from losing its accreditation, and he stopped the negative momentum the school had experienced.

The movie *Stand and Deliver* made it look as though Escalante was the one who came up with the idea of preparing students to take an advanced placement (AP) exam. The reality was that a few AP tests were already being given on campus. Each year several students took tests for Spanish. And occasionally, one or two would attempt a test in physics or history. But the problem was that the school didn't have a leader with vision to take up the cause. That's where Escalante came into play. He believed that he and the school could make a positive impact on his students' lives, and the way to start the ball rolling was to challenge the school's best and brightest with an AP calculus test.

In the fall of 1978, Escalante organized the first calculus class. Rounding up every possible candidate who might be able to handle the course from Garfield's three-thousand-five-hundred student population, he was able to find only fourteen students. In the first few classes, he laid out the work it would take for them to prepare for the AP calculus test at the end of the year.

At the end of the second week of school, he had lost seven students—half the class. Even the ones who stayed were not well prepared for calculus. And by late spring he was down to only five students. All of them took the AP test in May, but only two passed.

Escalante was disappointed, but he refused to give up, especially since he had made some progress. He knew that if he could give some of the students a few wins, build their confidence, and give them hope, he could start them moving forward. If he could just build some momentum, things at the school could turn around.

Escalante recognized that he could succeed only if his students were effectively inspired and properly prepared. Motivation would not be a problem because the calculus teacher was gifted in that area. He read his students masterfully and always knew exactly what to do with them. If they needed motivation, he'd give them extra homework or challenge one of the school's athletes to a handball match. (Escalante never lost!) If they needed encouragement, he'd take them out to McDonald's as a reward. If they got lazy, he'd inspire, amaze, amuse, and even intimidate them. And all along the way, he modeled hard work, dedication to excellence, and what he called *ganas*—desire.

Getting his students prepared was more difficult. He introduced more algebra and trigonometry to students in the lower-level classes, and he got some of his colleagues to do the same. He also started to rally support for a summer program to teach advanced math. And in time, the students got better.

In the fall Escalante put together another calculus class, this time with nine students. At the end of the year, eight took the test and six passed. He was making progress. Word of his success spread, and in the fall of 1980, his calculus class numbered fifteen. When they all took the test at the end of the year, fourteen students passed. The steps forward weren't huge, but Escalante could see that the program was starting to build momentum.

The next group of students, numbering eighteen, was the subject of the movie *Stand and Deliver*. Like their predecessors, they worked very hard to learn calculus, many coming to school at 7 A.M. every day—a full hour and a half before school started. And often they stayed until 5, 6, or 7 P.M. When they took the test in May, they felt that they had done well.

But then there was a problem, one that threatened to destroy the fledgling program and stop cold the momentum Escalante had been working hard to build over the past several years. A grader for the Educational Testing Service (ETS), which administered the AP exams, found some similarities on several of the tests the students had taken. That led to an investigation of fourteen of the eighteen Garfield students who took the test. The testers accused Escalante's students of cheating.

Resolving the investigation was a bureaucratic nightmare. The only way for the students to receive the college credit they wanted so desperately was to retake the test, but the students were indignant and felt retesting was an admission of guilt. Escalante tried to intervene, but the bureaucrats at ETS refused to talk with him. Henry Gradillas, who was then the principal, also tried to get the testing service to reverse their decision but was unsuccessful. They were at an impasse.

Finally the students agreed to retake the test—even though they had been out of school and hadn't studied for three months. And what were the results? Every single student passed. Escalante's pass rate for the year was 100 percent.

What could have killed the momentum Escalante had built at Garfield turned into a real momentum builder. Students at the school became more confident, and people within the community began to rally around Escalante and his program. And the publicity surrounding the test gave a push of momentum that made it possible for East Los Angeles College to start a summer program that Escalante wanted for his students.

After that, the math program exploded. In 1983 the number of students passing the AP calculus exam almost doubled, from eighteen to thirty-one. The next year it doubled again, the number reaching sixty-three. And it continued growing. In 1987, one-hundred-twenty-nine students took the test with eighty-five of them receiving college credit. Garfield High School in East Los Angeles, once considered the sinkhole of the district, produced 27 percent of all passing AP calculus test scores by Mexican-Americans in the entire United States.

The benefits of the *Law of Momentum* were felt by all of Garfield High School's students. The school started offering classes to prepare students for other AP exams. In time Garfield held regular AP classes in Spanish, calculus, history, European history, biology, physics, French, government, and computer science.

In 1987 nine years after Escalante spearheaded the program, over 325 AP examinations were taken by students at Garfield. And most incredibly, Garfield had a waiting list of over 400 students from areas outside its boundaries wanting to enroll. The school that was once the laughing stock of the district, and which had almost lost its accreditation, was now one of the top three inner city schools in the entire nation![1] That's the power of the *Law of Momentum.*

OBSERVE

It takes a leader to create momentum. Followers catch it. And managers are able to continue it once it has begun. But *creating* it requires someone who can motivate others, not who needs to be motivated.

1. *What obstacles did Escalante face at Garfield High School?*

2. *How did he create the momentum needed for the students to succeed and to grow the AP program?*

3. *How did the student body, not just those in his class, benefit from his actions?*

4. *What do you think would have happened if the eighteen students hadn't retaken the test?*

5. *Is your organization or department currently experiencing positive momentum?*

6. *What obstacles to momentum are you currently facing?*

7. *What will it take to overcome them?*

LEARN

Momentum really is a leader's best friend. In fact, sometimes it's the only difference between losing and winning. That's why in basketball games, for instance, when the opposing team scores a lot of unanswered points and starts to develop too much momentum, a good coach will call a time out. He knows that if the other team's momentum gets too strong, his team is likely to lose the game.

Momentum also makes a huge difference in organizations. When you have no momentum, even the simplest tasks can seem like insurmountable problems. But when you've got momentum on your side, the future looks bright, obstacles look small, and trouble seems temporary.

Momentum Makes Leaders Look Better Than They Are

When leaders have momentum on their side, people think they're geniuses. They look past shortcomings. They forget about the mistakes the leaders have made. Momentum changes people's perspective of leaders.

Momentum Helps Followers Perform Better Than They Are

When leadership is strong and there's momentum in an organization, people are motivated and inspired to perform at higher levels. They become effective beyond even their own hopes and expectations.

If you remember the 1980 U.S. Olympic hockey team, you know what I'm talking about. The team was good, but not thought to be good enough to win the gold medal. Yet that's what they did. Why? Because leading up to the championship game, they won game after game against very tough teams. They gained so much momentum that they performed beyond their own capabilities. And after they beat the Russians, they came home with the gold medal.

Momentum Is Easier To Steer Than To Start

Have you ever been water-skiing? If so, you know that it's harder to get up on the water than it is to steer once you're up there. Think about the first time you skied. Before you got up, the boat was dragging you along, and it probably seemed like your arms were going to give way as the water flooded against your chest and into your face. For a moment, you might have believed you couldn't hold onto the towrope any longer. But then the force of the water drove your skis up onto the surface, and off you went. At that point, you were able to make a turn with only a subtle shift of weight from one foot to another. That's the way the momentum of leadership works. Getting started is a struggle, but once you're moving forward, you can really start to do some amazing things.

Momentum Is the Most Powerful Change Agent

With enough momentum, nearly any kind of change is possible. That was true for Garfield High School, considered by many people to be a place with no hope, and it's true for any other organization. Momentum puts victory within reach.

EVALUATE

Rate your own leadership by placing the number 1, 2, or 3 next to each of the following statements: 1 = Never 2 = Sometimes 3 = Always

_______ 1. My organization experiences strong and productive momentum, resulting in measurable growth.

_______ 2. I am a self-starter, and I'm self-motivated.

_______ 3. I will "rock the boat" when necessary.

_______ 4. I continually "push" the organization to the next level.

_______ 5. The key leaders around me possess a sense of urgency about our primary objectives.

_______ 6. Our momentum is a result of people buying into the vision.

_______ 7. I know what causes momentum and how to keep the momentum going.

_______ 8. I insist on innovation over transformation and progress over analysis.

_______ 9. We face the problems in our organization.

_______ 10. I accept responsibility for the bottom-line results.

_______ 11. I have leadership confidence.

_______ 12. We have a strategic plan to enhance continued momentum.

_______ 13. My personal leadership style possesses high drive and a bias for action.

_______ 14. I attract other momentum makers.

_______ 15. When I'm the primary leader of my organization, I believe I am ultimately responsible to create and sustain momentum.

_______ 16. When we are not experiencing good momentum, I focus on reigniting the momentum, not on overanalyzing.

_______ 17. I am ready and willing to make tough decisions in order to create momentum.

_______ 18. I will take a stand publicly on tough issues in order to generate productive momentum.

_______ 19. I delegate and empower in such a way that it generates a sense of positive and productive teamwork.

_______ 20. My personality is an asset to creating and sustaining a positive and cheerful environment.

_______ **Total**

50 - 60 This is an area of strength. Continue growing as a leader but also spend time helping others to develop in this area.

40 - 49 This area may not be hurting you as a leader, but it isn't helping you much either. To strengthen your leadership, develop yourself in this area.

20 - 39 This is an area of weakness in your leadership. Until you grow in this area, your leadership effectiveness will be negatively impacted.

DISCUSS

Answer the following questions and discuss your answers when you meet with your mentoring group.

1. *How do leaders benefit from momentum?*

2. *How do followers benefit from momentum?*

3. *Do you agree with the author that "with momentum nearly any kind of change is possible"? Explain.*

4. *Describe the momentum in your organization.*

5. *Who are the momentum makers in your organization? What have they done recently to create momentum?*

6. *What would create additional momentum in the organization?*

7. *What are you doing to become a momentum maker?*

TAKE ACTION

Harry Truman once said, "If you can't stand the heat, get out of the kitchen." But for leaders, that statement should be changed to read, "If you can't make some heat, get out of the kitchen."

As the leader you need to look for ways your team can experience wins by accomplishing goals. First start with the smaller things you know they can achieve and gradually move them to larger goals that are more difficult. These accomplishments will build team momentum and allow your team to attempt and accomplish even more.

List the wins that your team will go after below. Start with the small goals and gradually move to larger goals. Be sure to celebrate each accomplishment as you achieve it to build morale.

Goals

1. ________________
2. ________________
3. ________________
4. ________________
5. ________________
6. ________________
7. ________________
8. ________________
9. ________________
10. ________________

17

THE LAW OF PRIORITIES

Leaders Understand That Activity Is Not Necessarily Accomplishment

Leaders never grow to a point where they no longer need to prioritize. Following the *Law of Priorities* is something that good leaders keep doing, no matter whether they're leading a small group, pastoring a church, running a small business, or leading a billion-dollar corporation.

READ

Examine the life of any great leader, and you will see him or her putting priorities into action. Every time Norman Schwarzkopf assumed a new command, he didn't just rely on his leadership intuition, he also reexamined the unit's priorities. When Lee Iacocca took over Chrysler, the first thing he did was reorder its priorities. When explorer Roald Amundsen succeeded in taking his team to the South Pole and back, it was due, in part, to his ability to set right priorities.

Successful leaders live according to the *Law of Priorities*. They recognize that activity is not necessarily accomplishment. But the best leaders seem to be able to get the *Law of Priorities* to work for them by satisfying multiple priorities with each activity. This actually enables them to increase their focus while reducing their number of actions.

One leader who was a master at that was one of my idols: John Wooden, the former head basketball coach of the UCLA Bruins. He's called the Wizard of Westwood because the amazing feats he accomplished in the world of college sports were so incredible that they seemed to be magical.

The greatest evidence of Wooden's ability to make the *Law of Priorities* work for him could be seen in the way he approached basketball practice. Wooden claimed that he learned some of his methods from watching Frank Leahy, the great former Notre Dame–football head coach. He said, "I often went to his [Leahy's] practices and observed how he broke them up into periods. Then I would go home and analyze why he did things certain ways. As a player, I realized there was a great deal of time wasted. Leahy's concepts reinforced my ideas and helped in the ultimate development of what I do now."

Friends who've been in the military tell me that they often had to "hurry up and wait." That seems to be the way some coaches work too. Their players are asked to work their hearts out one minute and then to stand around doing nothing the next. But that's not the way Wooden worked. His practices were different. He orchestrated every moment of practice and planned each activity with specific purposes in mind.

Every year, Wooden determined a list of overall priorities for the team, based on observations from the previous season. Those items might include objectives such as, "Build confidence in Drollinger and Irgovich" or "Use three on two continuity drill at least three times a week." Usually he had about a dozen or so items that he wanted to work on throughout the season. But Wooden also reviewed his agenda for his teams every day. Each morning, he and an assistant would meticulously plan the day's practice. They usually spent two hours strategizing for a practice that might not even last that long. He drew ideas from notes jotted on three-by-five cards that he always carried with him. He planned every drill, minute by minute, and recorded the information in a notebook prior to practice. Wooden once boasted that if you asked what his team was doing on a specific date at three o'clock in 1963, he could tell you precisely what drill his team was running.

Wooden always maintained his focus, and he found ways for his players to do the same thing. And his special talent was for addressing several priority areas at once. For example to help players work on their free throws—something that many of them found tedious—Wooden instituted a free-throw shooting policy during scrimmages that would encourage them to concentrate and improve instead of just marking time. The sooner a sidelined player made a set number of shots, the sooner he could get back into action. And Wooden continually changed the number of shots required by the guards, forwards, and centers so that team members rotated in and out at different rates. That way everyone, regardless of position or starting status, got experience playing together, a critical priority for Wooden's development of total teamwork.

The most remarkable thing about John Wooden—and the most telling about his ability to focus on his priorities—is that he never scouted opposing teams. Instead, he focused on getting his players to reach *their* potential. And he addressed those things through practice and personal interaction with the players. It was never his goal to win championships or even to beat the other team. His desire was to get each person to play to his potential and to put the best possible team on the floor. And of course Wooden's results were incredible. In over forty years of coaching, he had only *one* losing season—his first. And he led his UCLA teams to four undefeated seasons and a record ten NCAA championships.[1] Wooden is a great leader. He just might be the finest man to coach in any sport. Why? Because every day he lived by the *Law of Priorities.*

OBSERVE

Stephen Covey says, "A leader is the one who climbs the tallest tree, surveys the entire situation, and yells, 'Wrong jungle!'" You see, leaders know that the greatest success comes only when you focus on what really matters. Otherwise, you're just spinning your wheels.

1. *What did Wooden do to prepare for a team practice?*

2. *How do you think Wooden's disinterest in scouting other teams reflected on his team's performance?*

3. *Give an example of how "activity is not necessarily accomplishment."*

4. *How do you prepare so that you can maximize your effort?*

5. *Who in your organization or profession always seems to be "on track" with the right priorities? To what do you attribute that ability?*

LEARN

For the last ten years, I've used two guidelines to help me measure my activity and determine my priorities. The first is the Pareto Principle. The idea is: If you focus your attention on the activities that rank in the top 20 percent in terms of importance, that will give you an 80 percent return on your effort. For example, if you have ten employees, you should give 80 percent of your time and attention to your best two people. If your have 100 customers, the top twenty will provide you with 80 percent of your business. If your to-do list has ten items on it, the two most important ones will give you an 80 percent return on your time. If you haven't already observed this phenomenon, test it and you'll see that it really works out.

The second guideline is the three *R*s: requirement, return, and reward. To be effective, leaders must order their lives according to these three questions:

What Is Required?

We're all accountable to somebody, whether it's an employer, a board of directors, our stock holders, or someone else. For that reason, your list of priorities must always begin with what is required of you. If it's not necessary for you to do something personally, then it should be delegated or eliminated.

What Gives the Greatest Return?

As a leader, you should spend most of your time working in your areas of greatest strength. If something can be done 80 percent as well by someone else in your organization, delegate it. If a responsibility could *potentially* meet that standard, then develop a person to handle it.

What Brings the Greatest Reward?

Tim Redmond said, "There are many things that will catch my eye, but there are only a few things that will catch my heart." Those things which bring the greatest personal reward are the fire lighters in a leader's life. Nothing energizes a person the way passion does.

Every year I ask the key leaders of my organizations and myself these three questions. We review the past year and take a hard look at how effective we're being. Activity is not necessarily accomplishment. If we want to continue to be effective, we have to work according to the *Law of Priorities*.

EVALUATE

Rate your own leadership by placing the number 1, 2, or 3 next to each of the following statements: 1 = Never 2 = Sometimes 3 = Always

_______ 1. I know which of my responsibilities produce the greatest results.

_______ 2. I invest the majority of my time in the few areas of my responsibilities that produce the greatest results.

_______ 3. I enjoy my priority responsibilities more than the distractions.

_______ 4. The key leaders on my team are focused on their most productive areas.

_______ 5. I do my priority tasks before my nonpriority tasks.

_______ 6. If I don't know how to handle a top priority issue, I work on it instead of avoiding it.

_______ 7. I clearly know my number-one priority and am consistently focused on it.

_______ 8. I'm in a system or environment where I'm recognized and rewarded for what I am required to do.

_______ 9. I keep my list of top priorities short.

_______ 10. My personal gifts and skills match my top responsibilities.

_______ 11. I encourage the people on my team to be focused on their priorities.

_______ 12. My team knows the mission and is dedicated to advancing the mission.

_______ 13. At least quarterly, my key leaders and I meet to discuss and make sure we are all focusing on our priorities.

_______ 14. It is easy for me to say no to low-priority demands.

_______ 15. When something is no longer effective, I cut it from my schedule.

_______ 16. Overall, I am a highly disciplined person.

_______ 17. I will rearrange my schedule to accommodate the top priority.

_______ 18. If asked, the person I report to would say that I am focused and productive according to the top priorities of the organization's mission.

_______ 19. I invest 80 percent of my time into the top 20 percent of my priorities.

_______ 20. I have a productive and effective daily system in place to help keep me focused on my priorities.

_______ **Total**

50 - 60 This is an area of strength. Continue growing as a leader but also spend time helping others to develop in this area.

40 - 49 This area may not be hurting you as a leader, but it isn't helping you much either. To strengthen your leadership, develop yourself in this area.

20 - 39 This is an area of weakness in your leadership. Until you grow in this area, your leadership effectiveness will be negatively impacted.

DISCUSS

Answer the following questions and discuss your answers when you meet with your mentoring group.

1. *What gives you the greatest reward? Why?*

2. *What gives you the greatest return? Why?*

3. *Do you agree with the Pareto Principle that your top 20 percent produces 80 percent of your results? Explain.*

4. *How does your organization delegate responsibilities?*

5. *How do you currently prioritize your responsibilities?*

6. *How can you change to be sure you always focus your greatest effort on your top 20 percent?*

TAKE ACTION

It's easier to balance a schedule that has only a few things on it, but leaders and emerging leaders seldom have just a few things on their calendars. If you kept track of your events and projects last year, look back at your calendar. If you didn't keep a detailed calendar, try to list the trips you took, projects you worked on, and daily tasks that made up your year. Answer the following questions by referring to that information.

1. What is required of me?

____

____

____

2. What gives the greatest return?

____

____

____

3. What brings the greatest reward?

____

____

____

4. What tasks that do not bring a high return can I delegate to someone else?

____

____

____

5. What tasks that do not bring a high return can be stopped altogether?

____

____

____

6. How can I define my top 20 percent priorities?

____

____

____

7. How will I dedicate time, energy, and resources to these top priorities?

____

____

____

8. What rewards do I expect from focusing on my top priorities?

____

____

____

9. Who will I ask to keep me accountable to my top priorities, and how often will we discuss my priorities?

____

____

____

18

THE LAW OF SACRIFICE

A Leader Must Give Up to Go Up

Sacrifice is a constant in leadership. It is an ongoing process, not a one-time payment. And when leaders look back at their careers, they recognize that there has always been a cost involved in moving forward. Leaders who want continued success must live by the *Law of Sacrifice.*

READ

In the 1970s the Chrysler Corporation was declining rapidly. By 1978 its market share was down from 25 to a puny 11 percent, and things were just getting worse. The organization was headed for bankruptcy. Then in November of 1978, Chrysler brought aboard a new leader. His name was Lee Iacocca. He was a seasoned car man who had worked his way up through the ranks at Ford to become the president of the Ford Motor Company, the highest leadership position possible under chairman Henry Ford II. In all, Iacocca worked for Ford for thirty-two years. And when he left in 1978, the company was earning record profits, having made $1.8 billion in *each* of his last two years running the business.

When Chrysler approached Iacocca to come on board with them, it presented him with the opportunity—and the challenge—of a lifetime. John

Riccardo, then chairman of the board for Chrysler, recognized that the company needed strong leadership to survive, something he himself could not adequately provide. According to Iacocca, Riccardo knew that he was in over his head, so he wanted to bring in the former Ford man as President of Chrysler. In turn Riccardo would step aside in less than two years so that Iacocca could become Chairman and CEO. John Riccardo was willing to sacrifice himself for the good of the company. As a result, Iacocca would have the chance to realize a lifelong dream: becoming the top man at one of the big three.

Iacocca accepted the job, but it also started him down his own road of personal sacrifice. The first came in his finances. The salary he accepted at Chrysler was a little over half what he had earned as the president of Ford. The next sacrifice came in his family life. At Ford, Iacocca had always prided himself on the fact that he worked hard from Monday to Friday, but he always set aside Saturday, Sunday, and most Friday nights for his family. And when he came home from work at the end of the day, he left his troubles at the office.

But to lead Chrysler, he had to work almost around the clock. And on top of that, when he got home, he couldn't sleep. Iacocca later described the company as having been run like a small grocery store, despite its size. There were no viable financial systems or controls in place, production and supply methods were a mess, products were poorly built, and nearly all of the divisions were run by turf-minded vice presidents who refused to work as a team. As a result, morale was terrible throughout the company, customer loyalty was the worst in the business, and the company continued to lose money.

Iacocca understood that successful leaders have to maintain an attitude of sacrifice in order to turn around an organization. They have to be willing to do what it takes to go to the next level. One of the first things Iacocca did was fire thirty-three of the thirty-five vice presidents during a three-year period. But even then, things continued to get worse. The country was experiencing a terrible recession and interest rates were the highest they'd ever been. Then oil prices skyrocketed when the Shah of Iran was deposed in early 1979. Chrysler's market share fell to a horrible 8 percent. Despite all Iacocca's work, it seemed as if the *Law of Sacrifice* wasn't working.

Iacocca worked harder to rebuild the company by bringing in the very best leaders in the business, many of whom had retired from Ford. He cut every expense he could, and built on the company's strengths, but that still wasn't enough. Chrysler was clearly headed for bankruptcy. So Iacocca had to face the greatest personal sacrifice of all: He would go to the American government with his proverbial hat in his hand for loan guarantees.

At Ford, Iacocca had developed a reputation for being highly critical of any government involvement in business. So when he approached Congress for help, no one spoke very kindly about him. Iacocca later said,

> In the minds of Congress and the media, we had sinned. We had missed the market, and we deserved to be punished.
>
> And punished we were. During the congressional hearings, we were held up before the entire world as living examples of everything that was wrong with American industry. We were humiliated on the editorial pages for not having the decency to give up and die gracefully. . . . Our wives and kids were the butt of jokes in shopping malls and schools. It was a far higher price to pay than just closing the doors and walking away. It was personal. It was pointed. And it was painful.

Swallowing his pride was a great sacrifice for Iacocca, one that many top corporate executives never would have made. But it was a price he had to pay to save the company.

At least one sacrifice he made at that time received some positive press: Iacocca reduced his own salary to $1 a year. At the time he said, "Leadership means setting an example. When you find yourself in a position of leadership, people follow your every move." He followed that action with requests for others to make sacrifices. He asked Chrysler's top executives to take a 10 percent pay cut. Then he asked for—and received—concessions from the unions and the banks that were working with the automaker. For Chrysler to succeed, they would all make sacrifices together. And succeed they did. By 1982, Chrysler generated an operating profit of $925 million, the best in their history. And in 1983, the company was able to pay back its loans.[1]

Chrysler has continued to succeed and grow. They've fought their way back, and today they have a combined U.S. and Canadian market share of over 16 percent—double what it was in the early years when Iacocca took over. He has since retired, but it was his leadership that put Chrysler back on the map. Why? Because he modeled the *Law of Sacrifice.*

OBSERVE

What was true for Lee Iacocca is true for any leader. You have to give up to go up. The true nature of leadership is really sacrifice.

1. *What were some of the sacrifices Lee Iacocca made?*

2. *What sacrifice did John Riccardo make?*

3. *How could Chrysler have regained their market without following The Law of Sacrifice?*

4. *What sacrifices have leaders in your profession or area of service made? Have these sacrifices paid off?*

LEARN

Leaders who want to rise have to do more than take an occasional cut in pay. They have to give up their rights. As my friend Gerald Brooks says, "When you become a leader, you lose the right to think about yourself." For every person the nature of the sacrifice may be different. For example Iacocca's greatest sacrifices came late in his career. In the case of someone like former South African president F. W. DeKlerk, who worked to dismantle apartheid in his country, the cost was his career itself. The circumstances may change from person to person, but the principle doesn't. Leadership means sacrifice.

Leaders give up to go up. That's true of every leader regardless of profession. Talk to any leader and you will find that he or she has made repeated sacrifices. Usually, the higher that leader has climbed, the greater the sacrifices he's made. Effective leaders sacrifice much that is good in order to dedicate themselves to what is best. That's the way the *Law of Sacrifice* works.

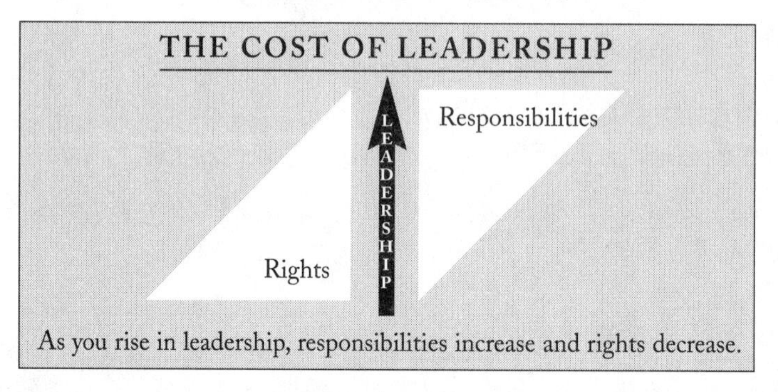

As you rise in leadership, responsibilities increase and rights decrease.

If leaders have to give up to go up, then they have to give up even more to stay up. Have you ever considered how infrequently teams have back-to-back championship seasons? The reason is simple: If a leader can take a team to the championship game and win it, he often assumes he can duplicate the results the next year without making changes. He becomes reluctant to make additional sacrifices in the off-season. But what gets a team to the top isn't what keeps it there. The only way to stay up is to give up even more. Leadership success requires continual change, improvement, and sacrifice. As philosopher-poet Ralph Waldo Emerson said, "For everything you have missed, you have gained something else; and for everything you gain, you lose something."

EVALUATE

Rate your own leadership by placing the number 1, 2, or 3 next to each of the following statements: 1 = Never 2 = Sometimes 3 = Always

_______ 1. I am willing to make significant sacrifices to grow as a leader.

_______ 2. I make significant sacrifices for the health and growth of my organization.

_______ 3. I make sacrifices without resenting the personal loss.

_______ 4. I will do whatever it takes to get the job done.

_______ 5. My peers would consider me a sacrificial leader.

_______ 6. I am clear and certain about the short list of sacrifices I'm not willing to make for the sake of my organization.

_______ 7. I find personal satisfaction and fulfillment in sacrifice for a worthy cause.

_______ 8. The key players on my team demonstrate that they are willing to sacrifice for the sake of the mission.

_______ 9. I see positive outcomes in our organization as a direct result from the sacrifices of many people.

_______ 10. I am willing to wait on the results, even when making a big sacrifice.

_______ 11. While leading the organization in seasons of sacrifice, I am able to genuinely maintain a cheerful and positive attitude.

_______ 12. I am willing to let go of what I have for the potential of something greater.

_______ 13. I understand and accept that sacrifice does not guarantee reward.

_______ 14. I am willing to make sacrifices for short and long periods of time.

_______ 15. Sacrifice for the greater good is part of my personal value system.

_______ 16. I am willing to lead the way by being the first to make sacrifices for the sake of our mission.

_______ 17. I expect more from myself than those I lead.

_______ 18. My personal sacrifices have inspired others to make personal sacrifices.

_______ 19. I view the principle of sacrifice as a lifestyle rather than a means to an end.

_______ 20. I anticipate that I will make more sacrifices as I grow as a leader.

_______ **Total**

50 - 60 This is an area of strength. Continue growing as a leader but also spend time helping others to develop in this area.

40 - 49 This area may not be hurting you as a leader, but it isn't helping you much either. To strengthen your leadership, develop yourself in this area.

20 - 39 This is an area of weakness in your leadership. Until you grow in this area, your leadership effectiveness will be negatively impacted.

DISCUSS

Answer the following questions and discuss your answers when you meet with your mentoring group.

1. *What is the premise for the Law of Sacrifice?*

2. *Do you agree that in order to move forward you will have to give something up? Explain.*

3. *Why do your rights decrease as your responsibilities increase?*

4. *Give an example of something you had to give up in order to reach a goal you set for yourself?*

5. *What have successful leaders in your organization given up in order to move forward or maintain their leadership?*

6. *What are the things that you will not give up?*

7. *What one thing could you give up today that would move you closer to a goal you have set for yourself? Explain how you will commit to sacrificing this thing.*

TAKE ACTION

The *Law of Sacrifice* can be seen in almost any diet or financial plan. You stop eating certain things to lose weight. You don't go to the movies every weekend so you can take the family on vacation in the summer. And just like food and money, time is also a commodity. Earl Nightingale says that if a person studied one hour a day for three years on a single topic, that he or she would become an expert in that field. But what would that person have to give up in order to spend the time studying?

This week, you are to find one thing in your life that if you give it up you believe it will move you forward. This is not limited to leadership. Moving forward might mean giving up your weekend golf game to spend more time with your family—investing in relationships. You could commit to waking up an hour earlier every morning to exercise—investing in your health. Or you could carve out one hour each day to learn about something that would advance your leadership and value to others—investing in your personal growth.

Fill in the blanks below, and commit to being committed!

For 6 months I will give up ________________________________
and instead I will ____________________________________

My goal is to ____

I will tell ______________________________________ about
my progress, and ask this person to keep me accountable.

19

THE LAW OF TIMING

When to Lead Is As Important As What to Do and Where to Go

When you understand the *Law of Timing* you'll begin to understand how certain things are possible. Leadership is not just about what to do and where to go; although, those two things are important. Sometimes a leader can make his or her biggest breakthrough by following the *Law of Timing*.

READ

When you understand the *Law of Timing*, you see why Jimmy Carter was elected President of the United States in 1976. In fact, Carter's life and career are characterized by one well-timed move after another. A graduate of Annapolis, Carter had intended to spend his career in the U.S. Navy, but when his father unexpectedly died in 1953, he returned to Plains, Georgia, to take over the family business. In only a few years, he became a strong, respected businessman and a leader in the community.

In 1962, times were changing, and Carter decided to run for the Georgia Senate. The old political machine in Georgia with its corrupt methods of electing officials was beginning to crumble. Carter recognized that for the first time in history, a person who was not part of the old system had a chance of being elected to office. But he faced a huge battle. The entrenched political bosses were still fighting to maintain control of their old turf. One corrupt leader openly intimidated voters in his district and falsified voting records. And as a result, Carter lost the primary. But he refused to quit without a battle. He fought the results of the primary and appealed to a superior court judge to have the voting process reviewed. When the results were overturned, Carter was able to stay on the ticket, and he went on to win the election. Then in 1970 he successfully ran for governor. Once again, he recognized that the timing was right for a relative newcomer to challenge the established political machine.

What Carter did next was almost unthinkable. He decided to run for President of the United States. Here was a man whose entire career as an elected politician consisted of one term in the Georgia Senate and one term as the state's governor. His experience was minimal, and he had no presence on the national scene. In fact Carter was such an unknown that when he appeared on the television show *What's My Line* in 1973, while governor, the panelists didn't know him nor could they guess his profession.

When Carter first threw his hat into the ring for the presidency, people in the media ignored him. They figured that a little-known ex-governor from the South with no Washington experience had no kind of chance to obtain the Democratic nomination, much less achieve the presidency. But Carter was undaunted. He and a few key associates had recognized that the timing would be right for him in 1976, and they met to talk about it. Carter biographer Peter G. Bourne, who attended the meeting, said that he saw "a unique, open opportunity for an outsider to run for the presidency." Carter saw it too; he knew that it was a now-or-never proposition.

Carter made his candidacy for president official in December of 1975, a year after finishing his term as governor. The reaction of people across the nation was painfully indifferent. Bourne said:

> Most journalists seemed not to grasp the profound social and political currents affecting the country. The impact of Vietnam, Watergate, the change in race relations in the South, and especially the profound opening up of the political process seemed largely ignored, and candidates were examined only within the context of the old political paradigm.[1]

The *Law of Timing* showed that it was the right time for an outsider to run, and Carter was everything that recent presidents had not been: He held no public office while campaigning, having finished his term as governor in 1974. He was not a lawyer by profession. He was a vocal proponent of his Christian faith. And unlike the people who had previously held the nation's highest office, he had not been a part of Washington politics as a congressman, senator, vice-president, or cabinet member. His was a fresh face with a different approach to government, something the American people desperately wanted. I believe that at no other time—either before or since—would Jimmy Carter have been elected. Remarkably, on January 20, 1977, James Earle Carter was inaugurated as thirty-eighth president of the United States.

However, timing was not always Jimmy Carter's friend. When the 1980 election rolled around, it killed his chances for reelection. The country faced as many problems as it ever had. The economy was a mess: Americans faced double-digit inflation, record-high oil prices, and skyrocketing mortgage rates. There were also numerous foreign-policy problems, including the Soviet invasion of Afghanistan and, of course, the long captivity of the American hostages in Iran. When a rescue attempt to free the captives was botched, it further worked against Carter. After the returns came in on the night of the election, Carter found that he had won only an abysmal forty-nine electoral votes to Ronald Reagan's 489. It was a devastating defeat. But the *Law of Timing* is a double-edged sword. Just as it served to elect Carter as president in 1976, it worked against him four years later.

OBSERVE

Reading a situation and knowing what to do are not enough to make you succeed in leadership. Only the right action at the right time will bring success.

1. *What made 1976 the right time for Jimmy Carter to run for President of the United States?*

2. *What made 1980's presidential race harder for Carter?*

3. *Do you agree with the author that Carter probably would not have been elected at any other time than 1976? Explain.*

4. *Give an example of how the Law of Timing has worked against someone in your profession or area of service.*

5. *What is happening in your profession or industry now that will require attention to timing?*

LEARN

Great leaders recognize that *when* to lead is as important as what to do and where to go. Every time a leader makes a move, there are really only four outcomes that can result. Take a look at them:

1. The Wrong Action at the Wrong Time Leads to Disaster

One of the worst things a leader can do is take the wrong action at the wrong time. When U.S. forces attempted to rescue the Iranian-held hostages during the Carter administration, it was an example of the wrong action at the wrong time. Prior to the decision to try the rescue, Secretary of State Cyrus Vance had argued that the plan was flawed. He believed something would go wrong. And of course, the attempt was a horrible failure. Several helicopters experienced mechanical problems, one got lost in a sand storm, and another crashed into a transport plane killing eight servicemen. Peter Bourne described it as "a combination of bad luck and military ineptitude." It could only be described as a disaster. It was an exercise in bad timing, and as much as anything else, it signaled the end of Carter's chances to be reelected.

2. The Right Action at the Wrong Time Brings Resistance

It's one thing to figure out *what* needs to be done; it's another to understand *when* to make a move. I remember a great example of this kind of bad timing from my own leadership experience. Back in the early 1980s, I tried to start a small-group program at Skyline, my church in San Diego. It was the right thing to do, but it failed miserably. Why? The timing was wrong. We hadn't recognized that we had developed too few leaders to support the launch. But six years later, when we tried again, the program was very successful. It was all a matter of timing.

3. The Wrong Action at the Right Time Is a Mistake

For about a decade, various colleagues of mine tried to talk me into doing a radio program. For a long time I resisted the idea. But a few years ago, I recognized that the time was right. So we created a program called *Growing Today.*

However, there was one problem: the format. I wanted to get materials into the hands of people to help them, but I was determined not to accept donations from the public. The solution, I thought, was to air a growth-oriented program and depend on product sales to support it. We found out that it was a mistake. That type of show just could not even break even. The timing was right, but the type of show was wrong.

THE RESULTS OF TIMING

ACTION

TIMING

Wrong Action Wrong Time ***Disaster***	Right Action Wrong Time ***Resistance***
Wrong Action Right Time ***Mistake***	Right Action Right Time ***Success***

4. The Right Action at the Right Time Results in Success

When leaders do the right things at the right time, success is almost inevitable. People, principles, and processes converge to make an incredible impact. And the results touch not only the leader, but also the followers and the whole organization.

When the right leader and the right timing come together, incredible things happen. Winston Churchill once said, "There comes a special moment in everyone's life, a moment for which that person was born. That special opportunity, when he seizes it, will fulfill his mission—a mission for which he is uniquely qualified. In that moment, he finds greatness. It is his finest hour." Churchill clearly understood the *Law of Timing*.

EVALUATE

Rate your own leadership by placing the number 1, 2, or 3 next to each of the following statements: 1 = Never 2 = Sometimes 3 = Always

_______ 1. As a leader I do the right things at the right time.

_______ 2. I talk to a small group of people, who serve as my inner circle of core advisors, before I make major decisions.

_______ 3. I not only think through the right thing to do, but invest time in thinking through the best process to make it happen.

_______ 4. Others trust my sense of timing.

_______ 5. I consider the past, present, and future when planning.

_______ 6. I have a high level of expertise in the area I'm responsible for making decisions in.

_______ 7. I can make the decisions that need to be made even when they involve intricate timing.

_______ 8. I thoroughly study the market conditions and critical trends before making major decisions or changes.

_______ 9. The timing errors I've made have been fixable.

_______ 10. I do my homework before making major decisions and recruiting key personnel.

_______ 11. I say the right thing at the right time.

_______ 12. I pay close attention to what other similar organizations are doing that is new and innovative.

_______ 13. Our organization does its best to create a realistic alignment of our visionary dreams and our financial resources.

_______ 14. When it comes to group interaction, I have a good internal sense of timing for what to do and what to say.

_______ 15. Other leaders seek my advice on issues of timing.

_______ 16. I connect the impact of current trends to my organization.

_______ 17. I am able to "close the deal" at the end of long negotiations.

_______ 18. I believe that choosing the right timing can be just as important as doing the right thing.

_______ 19. I am willing to hold off on making a change, even under tremendous pressure, if I'm confident that the timing is wrong.

_______ 20. After thinking through the best process for change, I seek council to confirm my inner sense of timing.

_______ **Total**

50 - 60 This is an area of strength. Continue growing as a leader but also spend time helping others to develop in this area.

40 - 49 This area may not be hurting you as a leader, but it isn't helping you much either. To strengthen your leadership, develop yourself in this area.

20 - 39 This is an area of weakness in your leadership. Until you grow in this area, your leadership effectiveness will be negatively impacted.

DISCUSS

Answer the following questions and discuss your answers when you meet with your mentoring group.

1. *What happens if you have the right idea, but you try to implement it at the wrong time?*

2. *What happens if you know it's time to do something, but choose the wrong thing to do? Give an example from your profession or area of service.*

3. *Do you agree with the author that your timing is just as important as what you do? Explain.*

4. *How has improper timing affected a leadership decision you were trying to implement?*

5. *Up until now, did you take timing into account when making a decision?*

6. *How do you think examining the timing of a decision will affect your leadership in the future?*

7. *What will you do to make sure that to the best of your ability your timing is right?*

TAKE ACTION

Some of the most intriguing movies contain plots that are enhanced by using the *Law of Timing*. Murder mysteries, westerns, and action adventure movies all rely on certain characters learning about what another character has done at a certain time, having the primary characters at a certain place at a certain time, and watching the hero take just the right steps at the right time in order to succeed.

This week, watch one of your favorite action movies. Take notes on how the *Law of Timing* played a role in success and failure. Record your comments below.

Law of Timing moment: ______________________________

What would have happened if the character had timed things differently?

Law of Timing moment: ______________________________

What would have happened if the character had timed things differently?

Law of Timing moment: ______________________________

What would have happened if the character had timed things differently?

____

____

____

Law of Timing moment: ___________________________

What would have happened if the character had timed things differently?

____

____

____

20

THE LAW OF EXPLOSIVE GROWTH

To Add Growth, Lead Followers—
To Multiply, Lead Leaders

Leaders who develop leaders experience an incredible multiplication effect in their organizations that can be achieved in no other way—not by increasing resources, reducing costs, increasing profit margins, analyzing systems, implementing quality management procedures, or doing anything else. As a leader you will go to the highest level only if you begin developing leaders instead of followers.

READ

In 1984 at age twenty-two, John Schnatter started his own business. He began by selling pizzas out of a converted broom closet at Mick's tavern, a lounge that was co-owned by his father. Although he was just a kid, he had a tremendous amount of vision, drive, and energy—enough to make that small pizza stand into a success. The next year, he opened his first store next door to Mick's in Jeffersonville, Indiana. He named the place Papa John's. For the next several years, Schnatter worked hard to build the company. In time, he opened additional stores, and later he began selling franchises. By the beginning of 1991, he had forty-six stores. That in itself is a great success story. But what happened during the next couple of years is even better.

In 1991 and 1992 Papa John's turned a huge corner. By the end of 1991, the number of stores more than doubled to 110 units. By the end of 1992, they had doubled again at 220. And the growth has continued dramatically. In early 1998 that number surpassed 1,600. What made the company suddenly experience such an incredible period of rapid expansion? The answer can be found in the *Law of Explosive Growth.*

Schnatter had always hired good people for his staff, but in the early years he was really the sole leader and primary driving force behind the business's success. Back in the 1980s, he didn't dedicate much time to developing other strong leaders. "It's taken a lot of growing on my part," says Schnatter of Papa John's success. "Between twenty-six and thirty-two [years old], the hardest thing was I had a lot of John Schnatters around me [people with great potential who needed to be mentored]. They needed a lot of coaching, and I was so busy developing myself, trying to get myself to the next level, I didn't develop those people. As a result, I lost them. It's my job to build the people who are going to build the company. That's going to be much harder for me than the first 1,200 stores."[1]

In the early 1990s Schnatter began thinking about what it would take to really grow the company. The key was leadership. He had already begun to grow as a leader personally. Having made significant progress on his own, his leadership development was now opening the door for him to attract better leaders to the company—and to give them the time they needed. That's when he started recruiting some of the people who would lead the company, including Wade Oney, who became the company's chief operating officer. Wade had worked for Domino's Pizza for fourteen years, and John believed he was one of the reasons their company had been so successful. When Wade left Domino's, John immediately asked him to be a part of the Papa John's Pizza team.

Schnatter had already built a company capable of creating a good pizza—and earning a healthy profit in the process. (Their per-store sales average is higher than Pizza Hut, Domino's, or Little Caesar's.) Now their goal was to build a bigger company. Together, they started talking about what it would take to be capable of opening four-hundred to five-hundred new restaurants a year. And that's when they began to focus their attention on developing leaders so that they could take the company to the next level. Says Oney, "The reason we're successful in the marketplace is our focus on quality and our desire to keep things simple. The reason we're successful as a company is our good people."

Since the early 1990s, Schnatter and Oney developed a top-rate team of leaders who helped the company experience explosive growth. Their growth has been phenomenal in an industry that was thought already to be glutted with competitors a decade ago. And Schnatter doesn't plan to stop growing his company until it's the largest seller of pizza in the world.

OBSERVE

Oney conveyed the *Law of Explosive Growth* by saying, "The challenge now, is developing the next leaders. The company's in great shape financially. [Acquiring] real estate is always a battle, but we can succeed there. And the economy is never a deterrent when you offer customers a good value. The key is to develop leaders. You do that by building up people."

1. *Why is leadership the key to growth?*

2. *What change did Schnatter make in the 1990s that allowed his company to experience explosive growth?*

3. *What organization in your field has experienced explosive growth and sustained growth? How did they grow so quickly?*

4. *What is the current focus in your organization: leading leaders or followers?*

LEARN

Any leader who practices the *Law of Explosive Growth* makes the shift from follower's math to what I call leader's math. Here's how it works. Leaders who develop followers grow their organizations only one person at a time. But leaders who develop leaders multiply their growth, because for every leader they develop, they also receive all of that leader's followers. Add 10 followers to your organization, and you have the power of 10 people. Add 10 leaders to your organization, and you have the power of 10 leaders times all the followers and leaders *they* influence. That's the difference between addition and multiplication. It's like growing your organization by teams instead of by individuals. The better the leaders you develop, the greater the quality and quantity of followers.

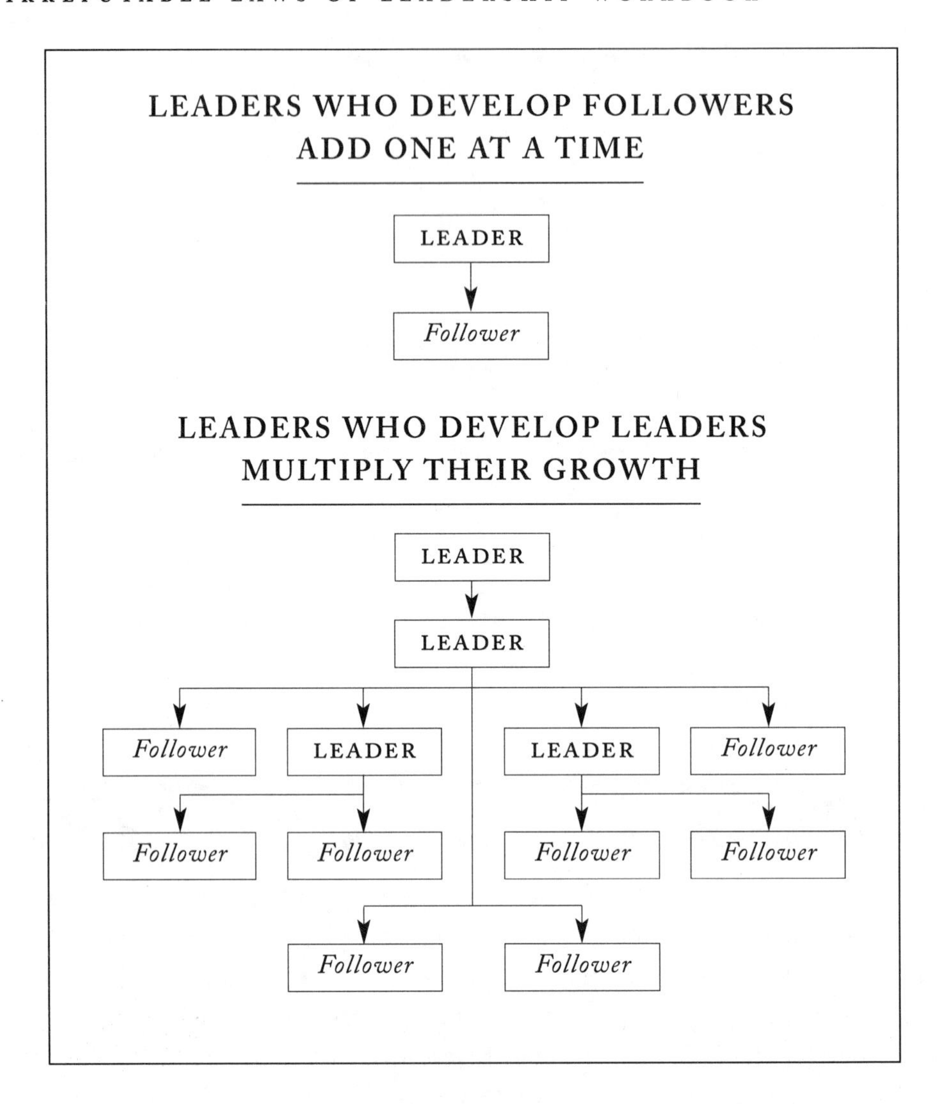

To go to the highest level, you have to become someone who develops leaders of leaders. As my friend Dale Galloway says, "Some leaders want to make followers. I want to make leaders. Not only do I want to make leaders, but I want to make leaders of leaders. And then leaders of leaders of leaders." Once you are able to follow that pattern, there's almost no limit to the growth your organization can experience. That's why I say that leaders who develop leaders multiply.

Becoming a leader who develops leaders requires an entirely different focus and attitude from that of a developer of followers. Take a look at some of the differences:

LEADERS WHO DEVELOP FOLLOWERS	LEADERS WHO DEVELOP LEADERS
Need to be needed	Want to be succeeded
Focus on weaknesses	Focus on strengths
Develop the bottom 20 percent	Develop the top 20 percent
Treat their people the same for "fairness"	Treat their leaders as individuals for impact
Hoard power	Give power away
Spend time with others	Invest time in others
Grow by addition	Grow by multiplication
Impact only those they touch personally	Impact people far beyond their own reach

Developing leaders is difficult because potential leaders are harder to find and attract. They're also harder to hold on to once you do find them, because unlike followers, they are energetic and entrepreneurial, and they tend to want to go their own way. Developing leaders is also hard work. Leadership development isn't an add-water-and-stir proposition. It takes time, energy, and resources.

EVALUATE

Rate your own leadership by placing the number 1, 2, or 3 next to each of the following statements: 1 = Never 2 = Sometimes 3 = Always

_______ 1. My organization experiences tremendous growth.

_______ 2. It is easy for others to see my contribution to our growth.

_______ 3. The growth of our organization is due largely to our leadership team.

_______ 4. Leadership training is available to people in our organization.

_______ 5. Our leadership-development opportunities are open to everyone in the organization.

_______ 6. We invest a generous amount of money into training.

_______ 7. Our training goes beyond the basic skills of a job.

_______ 8. We have identified the core values, skills, and characteristics that we want our leadership team to possess.

_______ 9. The environment of our organization is one of a thriving leadership culture.

_______ 10. We hire high-capacity people.

_______ 11. We hire people with a proven leadership track record and potential for future growth.

_______ 12. We do long-term training instead of fast-track training.

_______ 13. People in the organization show interest in the leadership training.

_______ 14. I am committed to my own personal growth, and I invest time at least weekly to my growth plan.

_______ 15. Our leaders are more concerned with building the organization than protecting their turf.

_______ 16. The leaders of the organization set an example by investing time in their own personal growth and the personal growth of those around them.

_______ 17. I am committed to doing whatever it takes to achieve maximum results.

_______ 18. We are first devoted to meeting our customers' needs, which in turn results in our organization's growth.

_______ 19. Our organization has a great reputation in the community.

_______ 20. Other organizations similar to ours look to us for help and ideas.

_______ **Total**

50 - 60 This is an area of strength. Continue growing as a leader but also spend time helping others to develop in this area.

40 - 49 This area may not be hurting you as a leader, but it isn't helping you much either. To strengthen your leadership, develop yourself in this area.

20 - 39 This is an area of weakness in your leadership. Until you grow in this area, your leadership effectiveness will be negatively impacted.

DISCUSS

Answer the following questions and discuss your answers when you meet with your mentoring group.

1. *What is leader's math?*

2. *Why do some leaders prefer to lead followers instead of leading leaders?*

3. *Do you agree with the author's description of leaders who develop followers and leaders who develop leaders? Explain.*

4. *Why would "being fair" not always be the right choice for a leader?*

5. *How has your organization's leadership contributed to the growth and progress of the company?*

6. *Would you consider yourself a follower, a leader of followers, or a leader of leaders? Explain.*

7. *How do you feel about being succeeded?*

8. *What attitude or views about leadership do you need to adjust in order to lead leaders?*

9. *What will you do to help your organization experience explosive growth?*

TAKE ACTION

One of the keys to leading leaders is being able to identify a person's leadership potential. Dale Carnegie, a master at identifying potential leaders, once said, "Men are developed the same way gold is mined. Several tons of dirt must be moved to get an ounce of gold. But you don't go into the mine looking for dirt. You go in looking for the gold."

This week use the following assessment to identify each of the potential leaders on your team. These are the people you want to spend time investing in and developing to become future leaders for your organization.

ASSESSMENT OF CURRENT LEADERSHIP QUALITIES

Scale

0=Never 1=Seldom 2=Sometimes 3=Usually 4=Always

1. The person has influence.	0	1	2	3	4
2. The person has self-discipline.	0	1	2	3	4
3. The person has a good track record.	0	1	2	3	4
4. The person has strong people skills.	0	1	2	3	4
5. The person does not accept the status quo.	0	1	2	3	4
6. The person has the ability to solve problems.	0	1	2	3	4
7. The person sees the big picture.	0	1	2	3	4
8. The person has the ability to handle stress.	0	1	2	3	4

9.	The person displays a positive spirit.	0	1	2	3	4
10.	The person understands people.	0	1	2	3	4
11.	The person is free of personal problems.	0	1	2	3	4
12.	The person is willing to take responsibility.	0	1	2	3	4
13.	The person is free from anger.	0	1	2	3	4
14.	The person is willing to make changes.	0	1	2	3	4
15.	The person has integrity.	0	1	2	3	4
16.	The person has a strong sense of self.	0	1	2	3	4
17.	The person has the ability to see what has to be done next.	0	1	2	3	4
18.	The person is accepted as a leader by others.	0	1	2	3	4
19.	The person has the ability and desire to keep learning.	0	1	2	3	4
20.	The person has a manner that draws people.	0	1	2	3	4
21.	The person has a good self-image.	0	1	2	3	4

22. The person has a willingness to serve others.	0	1	2	3	4
23. The person has the ability to develop other leaders.	0	1	2	3	4
24. The person has the ability to bounce back when problems arise.	0	1	2	3	4
25. The person takes initiative.	0	1	2	3	4

Total Points ____________

When assessing a potential leader, pay more attention to the quality of the person as addressed by the characteristics than to the specific score. Since leaders grade differently, scores vary. This is a general grading scale:

90–100 Great leader

80–89 Good leader

70–79 Emerging leader

60–69 Bursting with potential

Below 60 Needs growth but may not be ready to be mentored as a leader

Direct the 90–100 range people and ask them to mentor the 70–79 range people. Mentor the 80–89 range people yourself. Develop a leadership culture for the rest.

21

THE LAW OF LEGACY

A Leader's Lasting Value Is Measured by Succession

Every leader eventually leaves his organization. He may change jobs, get promoted, or retire. So a part of your job as a leader is to start preparing your people and organization for what inevitably lies ahead. That's where the *Law of Legacy* comes into play.

READ

In 1997 one of the finest business leaders in the world died. His name was Roberto Goizueta, and he was the chairman and chief executive of the Coca-Cola Company. In a speech he gave to the Executives' Club of Chicago a few months before he died, Goizueta made this statement: "A billion hours ago, human life appeared on Earth. A billion minutes ago, Christianity emerged. A billion seconds ago, the Beatles performed on 'The Ed Sullivan Show.' A billion Coca-Colas ago . . . was yesterday morning. And the question we are asking ourselves now is, 'What must we do to make a billion Coca-Colas ago this morning?'"

Making Coca-Cola the best company in the world was Goizueta's lifelong quest, one he was still pursuing diligently when he suddenly, unexpectedly died. Companies that lose a CEO often go into great turmoil, especially if his departure is due to an unexpected death, such as Goizueta's. Shortly before his death, Goizueta said in an interview with the *Atlanta Journal-Constitution* that retirement was "not on my radar screen. As long as I'm having the fun I'm having, as long as I have the energy necessary, as long as I'm not keeping people from their day in the sun, and as long as the board wants me to stay on, I will stay on." Just months after the interview, he was diagnosed with cancer. Six weeks later, he died.

Upon Goizueta's death, Former President Jimmy Carter said, "Perhaps no other corporate leader in modern times has so beautifully exemplified the American dream. He believed that in America, all things are possible. He lived that dream. And because of his extraordinary leadership skills, he helped thousands of others realize their dreams as well."

The legacy left to the company by Goizueta is incredible. When he took over Coca-Cola in 1981, the company's value was $4 billion. Under Goizueta's leadership, it rose to $150 billion. That's an increase in value of 3,500 percent! Coca-Cola became the second most valuable corporation in America, ahead of the car makers, the oil companies, Microsoft, Wal-Mart and all the rest. The only company more valuable was General Electric. Many of Coke's stockholders became millionaires many times over. Emory University in Atlanta, whose portfolio contains a large block of Coca-Cola stock, now has an endowment comparable to that of Harvard.

But high stock value wasn't the greatest thing Goizueta gave to the Coca-Cola Company. Instead it was the way he lived the *Law of Legacy*. When the CEO's death was announced, there was no panic among Coca-Cola stockholders. Paine Webber analyst Emanuel Goldman said that Goizueta "prepared the company for his not being there as well as any executive I've ever seen."

How did he do it? First, by making the company as strong as he possibly could. Second, by preparing a successor for the top position named Douglas Ivester. Mickey H. Gramig, writer for the *Atlanta Constitution,* said:

> Unlike some companies, which face a crisis when the top executive leaves or dies, Coca-Cola is expected to retain its status as one of the world's most admired corporations. Goizueta had groomed Ivester to follow his footsteps since the Georgia native's 1994 appointment to the company's number two post. And as an indication of how strongly Wall Street felt about Coca-Cola's

footings, the company's stock barely rippled six weeks ago when Goizueta was diagnosed with lung cancer.[1]

Doug Ivester, an accountant by training, started his career with Coca-Cola in 1979 as the assistant controller. Four years later, he was named chief financial officer. He was known for his exceptional financial creativity, and he was a major force in Goizueta's ability to revolutionize the company's approach to investment and the handling of debt. By 1989 Goizueta must have decided that Ivester had great potential, because he moved him out of his strictly financial role and sent him to Europe to get operating and international experience. A year later, Goizueta brought him back and named him president of Coca-Cola USA, where he oversaw expenditures and marketing. From there he continued to groom Ivester, and in 1994 there could be no doubt that Ivester would follow Goizueta into the top position. Goizueta made him president and chief operating officer.

What Roberto Goizueta did was very unusual. Few chief executives of companies today develop strong leaders and groom them to take over the organization. John S. Wood, a consultant at Egon Zehnder International Inc. says, "Companies have not in the recent past been investing as heavily in bringing people up. If they're not able to grow them, they have to go get them." So why was Roberto Goizueta different? He himself was a product of the *Law of Legacy*.

Roberto Goizueta was born in Cuba and educated at Yale, where he earned a degree in chemical engineering. When he returned to Havana in 1954, he answered a newspaper ad for a bilingual chemist. The company hiring turned out to be Coca-Cola. By 1966 he had become vice president of technical research and development at the company's headquarters in Atlanta. He was the youngest man ever to hold such a position in the company. But in the early 1970s, something important happened. Robert W. Woodruff, the patriarch of Coca-Cola, took Goizueta under his wing and began developing him. In 1975 Goizueta became the executive vice president of the company's technical division and took on other corporate responsibilities, such as overseeing legal affairs. And in 1980, with Woodruff's blessing, Goizueta became president and chief operating officer. One year later he was the chairman and chief executive. The reason Goizueta so confidently selected, developed, and groomed a successor is that he was building on the legacy that he had himself received in the 1970s.

OBSERVE

Of all the laws of leadership, the *Law of Legacy* is the one that the fewest leaders seem to learn. Achievement comes to someone when he is able to do great things for himself. Success comes when he empowers followers to do great things *with* him. Significance comes when he develops leaders to do great things *for* him. But a legacy is created only when a person puts his organization into the position to do great things *without* him.

1. *What legacy did Goizueta leave Coca-Cola?*

2. *How did Goizueta prepare Ivester to take his place?*

3. *Why wasn't Coca-Cola's stock affected when the leader became ill?*

4. *What organization similar to your own has had a significant leader leave? How did this affect the organization? Why?*

LEARN

Leaders who practice the *Law of Legacy* are rare. But the ones who do, leave a legacy of succession for their organization by doing the following:

1. Lead the Organization with a "Long View"

Just about anybody can make an organization look good for a moment—by launching a flashy new program or product, drawing crowds to a big event, or slashing the budget to boost the bottom line. But leaders who leave a legacy take a different approach. They lead with tomorrow in mind as well as today. That's what Goizueta did. He planned to keep leading as long as he was effective, yet he got his successor ready anyway. He always looked out for the best interests of the organization and its stockholders.

2. Create a Leadership Culture

The most stable companies have strong leaders at every level of the organization. The only way to develop such wide-spread leadership is to make developing leaders a part of your culture. That is a strong part of Coca-Cola's legacy. How many successful companies do you know about that have had a succession of leaders come up within the ranks of their own organizations?

3. Pay the Price Today to Ensure Success Tomorrow

There is no success without sacrifice. Each organization is unique, and that dictates what the price will be. But any leader who wants to help his or her organization must be willing to pay that price to ensure lasting success.

4. Value Team Leadership Above Individual Leadership

No matter how good he or she is, no leader can do it all alone. Just as in sports a coach needs a team of good players to win, an organization needs a team of good *leaders* to succeed. The larger the organization, the stronger, larger, and deeper the team of leaders needs to be.

5. Walk Away from the Organization with Integrity

In the case of Coca-Cola, their leader didn't get the opportunity to walk away because he died an untimely death. But if he had lived, I believe Goizueta would have done just that. When it's a leader's time to leave the organization, he's got to be willing to walk away and let his successor do his own thing. Meddling only hurts him and the organization.

Goizueta once said, "Leadership is one of the things you cannot delegate. You either exercise it, or you abdicate it." There is also a third choice: you pass it on to your successor. That's a choice Goizueta exercised, and it's the choice all leaders should make.

EVALUATE

Rate your own leadership by placing the number 1, 2, or 3 next to each of the following statements: 1 = Never 2 = Sometimes 3 = Always

_______ 1. I am committed to investing my life into other people.

_______ 2. I focus my talents and energy in such a way that they will benefit those who come after me.

_______ 3. I invest a portion of my time into those who are younger than I am.

_______ 4. My contributions benefit others.

_______ 5. I invest my time in bettering the future of others rather than ensuring my own security.

_______ 6. My work is more fulfilling than frustrating.

_______ 7. I have settled the issue of what area my greatest contribution to the world will be in.

_______ 8. My primary responsibilities are utilizing my greatest gifts.

_______ 9. I find great personal joy in identifying people with potential and investing my life into them.

_______ 10. I tend to be more of a team player than a solo player.

_______ 11. There is clear evidence of both my productiveness and happiness at work.

_______ 12. I view life with a "larger-than-me" perspective.

_______ 13. I invest my life into others with a vision of helping them do what they do better.

_______ 14. The legacy I'm committed to is about the benefit of others, not stockpiling for myself.

_______ 15. Other people are attracted to the legacy I want to leave and want to help me make a difference.

_______ 16. I am willing to invest myself in returns that I may never personally realize.

_______ 17. My dreams and desires about leaving a legacy involve the organization and are not for my personal benefit.

_______ 18. It is easy for me to share power and control.

_______ 19. I live my life to reflect the principle that says it's more important for people to live better than for my name to be remembered.

_______ 20. I can clearly cast the vision for the legacy that I wish to leave the organization.

_______ **Total**

50 - 60 This is an area of strength. Continue growing as a leader,but also spend time helping others to develop in this area.

40 - 49 This area may not be hurting you as a leader, but it isn't helping you much either. To strengthen your leadership, develop yourself in this area.

20 - 39 This is an area of weakness in your leadership. Until you grow in this area, your leadership effectiveness will be negatively impacted.

DISCUSS

Answer the following questions and discuss your answers when you meet with your mentoring group.

1. *Why are leaders who practice the Law of Legacy rare?*

2. *Why does an organization need a team of good leaders to succeed?*

3. *What are the advantages of promoting people into leadership positions from within your organization instead of recruiting leaders from other organizations?*

4. *What does your organization's potential legacy look like? Who is involved in building that legacy?*

5. *What priority have you placed on mentoring others? Explain.*

6. *How would you go about choosing someone to replace yourself?*

7. *If you suddenly left your organization, what would the impact be?*

8. *What is your attitude when asked to teach someone in the organization a skill that you know? Why is this your reaction?*

9. *What will you do to ensure the legacy and future success of your organization?*

TAKE ACTION

People invest in what they believe in. And if you are just half-hearted about the organization you work for, it is unlikely that you will invest in that organization's future. Spend at least an hour today brainstorming and recording your thoughts below about why you do what you do. At the end of this time you may realize that you need to move into something that will better suit your gifts and talents, an organization that you will willingly invest in. You may realize that you are right where you need to be, and that you should be investing in the vision and future of this organization. Or you may see how your current position is just a stepping-stone on your journey, but you can still invest by improving yourself as you try to strengthen the organization.

Some questions to get you started:

1. What does my organization provide for the community?

2. Why is my organization important?

3. I believe in my organization's mission statement because

4. The job I think I would most enjoy would be

5. I do what I do because ________________________________

____

____

____

6. When all is said and done, I want my impact to be __________

____

____

____

NOTES

CHAPTER 1

1. John F. Love, *McDonald's: Behind the Arches* (New York: Bantam Books, 1986).

CHAPTER 2

1. Thomas A. Stewart, "Brain Power: Who Owns It . . . How They Profit from It," *Fortune*, 17 March 1997, 105–6.

CHAPTER 3

1. "The Champ," *Readers Digest*, January 1972, 109.
2. Milton Meltzer, *Theodore Roosevelt and His America* (New York: Franklin Watts, 1994).

CHAPTER 4

1. *Forbes.*

CHAPTER 6

1. Robert S. McNamara with Brian VanDeMark, *In Retrospect: The Tragedy and Lessons of Vietnam* (New York: Times Books, 1995).
2. E. M. Swift, "Odd Man Out," *Sports Ilustrated*, 92–96.
3. Robert Shaw, "Tough Trust," *Leader to Leader* (Winter 1997), 46–54.

CHAPTER 7

1. M. W. Taylor, *Harriet Tubman* (New York: Chelsea House Publishers, 1991).

CHAPTER 10

1. H. Norman Schwarzkopf, "Lessons in Leadership," Vol. 12, no.5.

CHAPTER 11

1. Warren Bennis, *Scarce Organizing Genius: The Secrets of Creative Collaboration.*
2. Judith M. Bardwick, *In Praise of Good Business* (New York: John Wiley and Sons, 1988).

CHAPTER 12

1. Lee Iacocca and William Novak, *Iacocca: An Autobiography* (New York: Bentam Books, 1984).

CHAPTER 15

1. James C. Humes, *The Wit and Wisdom of Winston Churchill* (New York: Harper Perennial, 1994).
2. Arthur Schlesinger Jr., "Franklin Delano Roosevelt," *Time*, 13 April 1998.

CHAPTER 16

1. Jay Mathews, *Escalante: The Best Teacher in America* (New York: Henry Holt, 1988).

CHAPTER 17

1. John Wooden and Jack Tobin, *They Call Me Coach* (Chicago: Contemporary Books, 1988).

CHAPTER 18

1. Lee Iacocca and William Novak, *Iacocca: An Autobiography* (New York: Bantam Books, 1984).

CHAPTER 19

1. Peter G. Bourne, *Jimmy Carter: A Comprehensive Biography from Plains to Postpresidency* (New York: Scribner, 1997).

CHAPTER 20

1. Rajan Chaudhry, "Dough Boy," *Chain Leader*, April 1997.

CHAPTER 21

1. Mickey H. Gramig, *Atlanta Constitution*, 10 November 1997.

ABOUT THE AUTHOR

JOHN C. MAXWELL, known as America's expert on leadership, is founder of the INJOY Group, an organization dedicated to helping people maximize their personal and leadership potential. Each year Maxwell speaks in person to more than 350,000 people and influences the lives of more than one million people through seminars, books and tapes. He is the bestselling author of more than twenty-five books, including *The 21 Irrefutable Laws of Leadership*, *Failing Forward*, *Developing the Leader Within You*, and *The 21 Indispensable Qualities of a Leader*.

STEP 3 Take your leadership training—and that of your team—to the next level. Purchase the complete audio (for your personal use) and video (for group training) *21 Laws* series and maximize your leadership potential!

Living the 21 Irrefutable Laws of Leadership

Audio Program
John C. Maxwell

You will achieve more than you ever imagined by simply listening to one leadership lesson, reading one chapter, and completing one assignment each month. With *Living the 21 Laws,* you'll have a leadership growth tool that will allow you to:

- **Evaluate your leadership strengths**
- **Create a proactive plan to improve your leadership skills**
- **Understand the laws so that you can readily teach them**

This exceptional package includes:

- **12 audiocassettes containing 21 lessons**
- **A complete personal development manual**

Learning the 21 Irrefutable Laws of Leadership

Video Program
John C. Maxwell

How do you propel your organization to a new level? Make sure that you are all growing together! These dynamic videos will allow you to bring your entire leadership team together to develop a shared vision, a corporate purpose, and a unified effort. Plus, it will make teaching easier and less time consuming for you.

Package contents:

- **5 interactive videos**
- **1 complete set of outlines and notes**
- **1 copy of the best-selling book, *The 21 Irrefutable Laws of Leadership***
- **1 bonus introductory video**

Maximum Impact™ is dedicated to developing you as a leader of excellence and integrity by providing the finest resources and training for your personal and professional growth. Visit www.maximumimpact.com *often for the best in leadership training materials and continue to grow your influence!*

The INJOY Group™
A Lifelong Partner Dedicated to Lifting Your Potential

The INJOY Group™, founded in 1985 by Dr. John C. Maxwell, dedicates itself to adding value to individuals and organizations across America and around the world. It accomplishes its mission by forging lasting partnerships that foster personal growth and organizational effectiveness.

The INJOY Group™ consists of . . .

INJOY® Resources—Equipping People to Succeed

INJOY® Conferences—Empowering Leaders to Excel

INJOY® Stewardship Services—Energizing Churches to Raise Funds for Financing the Future

EQUIP™—Affecting Leadership Development in Emerging Countries, American Urban Centers, and Academic Communities

Each year, The INJOY Group™ partners with tens of thousands of people, dozens of church denominations, and countless business and nonprofit organizations to help people reach their potential.

To learn more about Dr. John C. Maxwell or any division of The INJOY Group™, visit us at:

www.INJOY.com

Books by Dr. John C. Maxwell Can Teach You How to Be a REAL Success

RELATIONSHIPS

Be a People Person (Victor Books)
Becoming a Person of Influence (Thomas Nelson)
The Power of Influence (Honor Books)
The Power of Partnership in the Church (J. Countryman)
The Treasure of a Friend (J. Countryman)

EQUIPPING

Developing the Leaders Around You (Thomas Nelson)
Partners in Prayer (Thomas Nelson)
Your Road Map for Success (Thomas Nelson)
Your Road Map for Success Workbook (Thomas Nelson)
Success One Day at a Time (J. Countryman)
The 17 Indisputable Laws of Teamwork (Thomas Nelson)
The 17 Essential Qualities of a Team Player (Thomas Nelson)

ATTITUDE

Be All You Can Be (Victor Books)
Failing Forward (Thomas Nelson)
The Power of Thinking (Honor Books)
Living at the Next Level (Thomas Nelson)
Think on These Things (Beacon Hill)
The Winning Attitude (Thomas Nelson)
Your Bridge to a Better Future (Thomas Nelson)
The Power of Attitude (Honor Books)

LEADERSHIP

The 21 Indispensable Qualities of a Leader (Thomas Nelson)
The 21 Irrefutable Laws of Leadership (Thomas Nelson)
The 21 Most Powerful Minutes in a Leader's Day (Thomas Nelson)
Developing the Leader Within You Workbook (Thomas Nelson)
Developing the Leader Within You (Thomas Nelson)
The Power of Leadership (Honor Books)
The Right to Lead (J. Countryman)

WORKBOOK NOTES

WORKBOOK NOTES

WORKBOOK NOTES

WORKBOOK NOTES

WORKBOOK NOTES

WORKBOOK NOTES

WORKBOOK NOTES